A Pig's Tale

A Pig's Tale

SURVIVAL IS AS MUCH A MATTER OF GRACE AS FIGHT

" Survival is as much a matter of grace as fight."

—GRETEL EHRLICH

ABBY VEGA

PALMETTO
PUBLISHING
Charleston, SC
www.PalmettoPublishing.com

Paperback ISBN: 979-8-8229-3844-1
eBook ISBN: 979-8-8229-3845-8

Contact Abby Vega:
Vega Family Enterprises
Vabby2813@gmail.com
(904) 610-6294

ABBY VEGA PRAISES FOR:

A PIG'S TALE!

A very clever and creative perspective on the challenges of building a professional team under less than optimal circumstances. The fundamentals of good leadership and continuous problem solving are illustrated in a fun and unique tale that humorously captures the nuances of managing people. This delightful book by Abby Vega is a gem for anyone looking to broaden their perspective on effective management skills without losing sight of what really matters in becoming successful.

—AMY BIXLER, PSY.D, HSPP

I have had the good fortune of knowing Abby for well over forty years, since I was in high school. With great joy, I can also say that we have been friends all of these years.

We share countless memories of meaningful conversations, bowling, my losing at Scrabble, naming that tune on car trips, and my frustration in never being able to remember her favorite song group's name, Spiral Staircase. The song is "I Love You More Today Than Yesterday." We have memories of vacations, making kruschiki, (Polish Bow Cookies), our weddings, babies, funerals—you get the picture, over forty years of life. Through the many seasons and events in our lives, one thing has remained consistent: Abby is who Abby is—hard- working, generous, resilient, focused, determined, smart, and funny.

*She is passionate and has an inner drive, always
seeking to challenge herself to be her best self and always
wanting the best for those in her life. Always!*

*Abby also has the rare quality of living and leading with both
her head and her heart, and I have much admiration for her in
this regard. I believe many are gifted with both capabilities, but
few have the courage to wake up every day and operate in both.
Abby always does, and this is best showcased in her story of "A Pig's
Tale." Her heart is always about giving back and helping loved
ones, friends, colleagues, and even strangers, as also evidenced in
her first book, "Sno Cone Diaries." I know she has done it for me
personally and for so many countless others innumerable times.*

*I'm honored to know Abby and forever grateful for our friendship.
We both enjoy music. The lyrics from the song "Thank You for
Being a Friend" by Andrew Gold, describe my friend perfectly.*

—TRISH NEUBAUER

*I had the distinct honor of working with Abby Vega in a corporate
job for two and a half years until the dissolution of our division
due to the impacts of Covid-19. It was that experience that forged
our friendship, and that is where I experienced her magic, which I
affectionately named the "Abby Factor." Not only did she bring the
Abby Factor to our organization and the mission we were tasked
with achieving during Covid, she also helped me tap into my own
magic. Since we were all working from home, we had a call over
coffee every morning to strategize about how we could create magic
that day. We laughed together, cried together, and we made our
Magic! We faced the challenges of launching a new product during
a pandemic but never let that dim our light. We coined the phrase
"The Magic of Eight." It symbolizes selling a year's supply to assist*

doctors in keeping their patients healthy in an unprecedented time in history when everything was being ordered online, and we brought that to every interaction we had, both internal and external, until the end of our corporate journey. This book is such a true depiction of the measure of woman that she is. One of the most beautiful characteristics Abby carries is her true heart to not only succeed individually but to encourage and elevate those around her, both through her honesty and integrity as well as her generous heart. I am so blessed to call her a true friend and excited to see her heart reach out to so many others through A Pig's Tale!

—HEATHER POUNCEY, FRIEND, CO-WORKER, AND MAGIC OF EIGHT CO-INSTIGATOR

Isabel M. Steiner

CAN YOU TEACH A PIG FLY?

Is it really possible to teach a pig to fly?
Chimera, the experts adamantly imply!
For it wastes your time and frustrates the pig,
Says the self-righteous, moralistic prig!

Has anyone even considered the possibilities if they did?
Oh, the endless potentiality, Heaven forbid!
Their wings are the knowledge. And resolution to win is their will,
Their fuselage is their truth upon which they have built this skill.

So pigs will fly, just you wait and see,
With dignity, purpose, passion, and a special grace, you'll agree.

—GRACE FULLY

DEDICATION

This book is dedicated to all the team members I've had the pleasure to manage over my long career in business. Thank you for making my job fun, challenging, and an opportunity for personal and professional growth—never dull or boring, and for the most part very satisfying and fulfilling. Thank you for the lifelong friendships, the memories, the wins, the losses, the doubts, the faith shown in me, and finally the endless material for stories to tell for many years to come. It was all worth it! Together through the good and the bad, we accomplished great things—not once, not twice, but over and over again, in many different companies, with very diverse cultures, outrageous sales goals and expectations, shaky business practices, good and bad senior leadership, and with teammates that sometimes were all on board and sometimes not at all. Letting people go was the hardest part of my job and the part I hated the most, but sometimes it needed to be done to make the teams stronger. Each and every one of you holds a special place in my heart because of the many exceptional moments that we had the privilege to share.

In all honesty, leadership can suck big time. No one in their right mind would sign up for leadership if they knew the pain that would be involved.

> *A true leader has the confidence to stand alone, the courage*
> *to make decisions, and the compassion to listen to the needs of*
> *others. One does not set out to be a leader, but becomes one by*
> *the equality of their actions, and the integrity of their intent*
>
> **—DOUGLAS MACARTHUR**

And yet I want you to know that when asked to lead, I always tried to be the best manager I could be. For the first team I managed, my promotion literally happened overnight, where one day I was a salesperson reporting to my manager, and then literally the next day I was promoted to manager with my former manager now reporting to me as a salesperson. Tricky and challenging circumstances to start with, but still an opportunity for the team to shine. And remember also at that time, my initial management training came only from my own personal experiences—more of a "what not to do if I ever get to be a manager" approach. My hope is that I grew into a manager you'd look back on fondly and think, "Working with Abby changed my life, my career, my outlook on whether management was a good option for me in the future," or even something like, "Now this is a person that gets it, preaches it, lives it and stands up for it.

She's got my back! She makes coming to work worthwhile! I trust her and believe in her; therefore, I will do my best to not disappoint her or my teammates."

I will never forget my first hire. I immediately had to find someone to replace me in my territory. I interviewed lots of people but kept coming back to this one young man who, despite being less experienced than other candidates, won me over because I didn't always ask conventional interview questions. I asked questions that looked into your heart and soul, your fears and motivations. When this young man told me his personal story of losing his mom as a young boy of eight and then, after reuniting with his dad, losing him also to death when he was just in his early twenties, I knew he would go on to do great things. I knew because he was a lot like me, in that he was hungry and had overcome some adversity and hardship, which gave him the desire and skills to be willing to do whatever it took to be successful. I got a lot of pushback on my decision, but he never let me down, and years later he flew to Jacksonville, took me to dinner, and thanked me for seeing what was possible and believing in him. Taking that chance allowed him to provide for his family and boost his career to take him to great things.

"Everyone needs someone to believe in them
until they can believe in themselves."

—ABBY VEGA

Every team is different because the cultures, the people and the challenges of each organization are unique. The key to being a successful manager is adapting your style to culturally fit in without sacrificing the real truth of who you are at heart and in your soul.

I knew that my commitment to staying true to my people was what drove them hardest to be successful. We worked hard, but we always took time to play. Playing always gave me a different perspective on who the person was outside of work and more insight into them if they interacted differently with their peers in a social setting. It would often confirm my initial beliefs about them, reveal weaknesses, or in some cases untruths, that I could then identify and address, strengthening the whole team because of what took place.

The important thing to take away from the tale in this book is how to deal with all these different types of people, cultures, leaders, issues, and challenges and still be a winner by practicing my Six Ground Rules of Leadership.

SIX GROUND RULES OF LEADERSHIP:

1. Stay true to who you are.

2. Practice what you preach.

3. Love your team.

4. Stand up for your team and show your strength, courage, and fortitude.

5. Always put your team's success before your own.

6. And if necessary, be willing to take a bullet for your team to earn their trust. That way, they know you aren't asking them to do something you wouldn't do yourself.

The most exacting team I ever managed was made up of fifteen men with four different areas of business expertise. Of the four areas of expertise mentioned, I personally had experience in only one of them, and I was hired as an outsider, and I was female. How could I convince them I was qualified to lead them and make them better at their jobs? It wasn't an easy go in the beginning, but once we all trusted that everyone was competent in their own roles, and that we could rely on each other in the other roles, we made lots of money, won awards, and kicked butt! I was initially given the nickname of "Darth Vega" until everyone was convinced through our individual and team successes that my role was truly not to be a villain but rather a heroine in their story.

All of these people I have been blessed to cross paths with are the inspiration for this tale, and they were the guinea pigs, if you will, for me trying to test all that I had learned in managing people and seeing if I could develop the quintessential formula to reach heights of success that would ultimately result in a leadership plan that could "teach a pig how to fly."

TABLE OF CONTENTS

FOREWORD

Grace Fully has been the most inspiring manager I have had the pleasure of working with. She encompassed the top leadership skills of relationship building, innovation, creativity, and employee motivation and took it to an extraordinary level. The team was given the opportunity to participate in the interview process, and everyone on the team was prepared with a designated question. Afterward, several team members were opposed to her being hired due to her lack of knowledge in aeronautics. When she was hired, she was adamant that she could manage us without that knowledge. Grace's primary goals were to identify our potential, develop our skills, and help us to reach our career goals. We knew how to do our jobs, and she was there to escalate issues and remove any barriers to us doing our jobs.

Grace came in to manage a team that was in its infancy and had been working independently without a direct manager for the majority of a year. Our department was one that most people didn't even know existed, much less who we served. It was a department where each staff member worked in his or her own silo and had little to no interaction with other departments. We started off with a broken foundation, but we repaired it and built something grand and unexpected, both individually and as a team. In short order we became the "Golden Team" that everyone wanted to be a part of.

With staff in two different locations, we had a quarterly team building session that was not your standard boring corporate team building exercise either. We had a theme, and everything we did tied into that theme in some way. Whether it was painting with a twist, personality tests, a drum circle, kayaking, or volunteering to help sick children and their families at Christmas time, I participated in things I never would have dreamed of— and I always walked away having learned something new about myself, my team, and my manager.

The personality test we took was very detailed and informative in outlining our strengths and weaknesses. Grace took that information and gave us opportunities to work in our strongest areas, but she also constantly challenged us to work on our weaknesses. One of my own personal weaknesses was small talk or initiating conversations. I feel socially awkward and consider myself an introvert. I used the fundraising initiative we were assigned as an opportunity to come out of my shell, and I challenged myself to approach colleagues and businesses to donate time, products, and services to help us exceed our goal. The personality test helped me identify many things I already knew about myself, but more importantly it showed me how I was being perceived by others. Now I am aware that I have to make a conscious effort when speaking with others to stop what I am doing and give my undivided attention to the person I am engaging with so that I am perceived as an interested and active listener. In my role then and now, I have to engage with customers constantly—something I never wanted and never thought I could be good at. Many of the people skills I have developed are a result of Grace Fully's influence and mentoring.

In one of the many team-building exercises we had, Grace gave everyone a journal and asked each of us to write down six things we wanted to accomplish. After we completed writing these down, we were given one die to roll. Whatever number we rolled, we were challenged to work specifically on that goal. To this day, I still get a journal every year and keep it with me to document my feelings and personal goals for fitness, work, travel and entertainment.

But of course, my biggest memory as well as my biggest personal challenge was our kayaking team-building adventure. Grace wanted to plan something on the water, but she knew that I was the only team member that couldn't swim. She often posed random questions to gauge my comfort level and then finally shared with me what she was thinking. I gave her the green light. But imagine my surprise when our guide pulled out kayaks and continuously stressed all the dangers associated with what we were about to do. Just as I was accepting that the life vest would prevent me from drowning, the guide would review other pitfalls to be aware of that were completely up to just me.

We went through the team-building part, which was only a little offshore, and someone was giving us verbal instructions and determining if they communicated the information to us in a way that could be understood in order for the team to deliver what was intended. Not surprisingly, as a team with our kayaks tied together, we achieved the goal, but on the return trip we were separated and had the opportunity to kayak solo. That didn't work out quite as well for the one person who couldn't swim and didn't know how to use the oars to steer in the right direction. While everyone was going to the right, I was drifting further downstream, abandoned, alone, and afraid. Eventually, with the team cheering me on from shore, I made it back safely, but that will remain the scariest, most challenging, and most fun adventure of my life.

I still have most of the items from our team-building experiences. My piggy bank and big pig portrait always occupy my office space, even though I have moved on to do other great things. I continue to use my ice cream scooper, and the little glass flying pig is always either in my desk drawer or in my wallet.

Grace has been the most inspirational leader and mentor. She was always completely transparent with us. Even though I reported to her as my manager, she made me feel like I was on her level and that my voice, my ideas, and my concerns were welcomed and validated.

Grace will always be the person I aspire to be.

—GUINEA STEFANI (GWIN)
TEAM LEAD: HOG DAWG
4/27/2023

INTRODUCTION

With all my heart, I believe I was born and placed on this earth to live, work, and share the love and learnings from this pig's tale. It is important that whenever you take on important new tasks where you want to be successful that you learn to **Commit like the Pig!**

> *"When you eat eggs and bacon, the chicken participates and the pig is committed."*
>
> **—MIKE LEACH**

Once you decide to commit to something work like bacon and **Be All In!**

It is my desire that reading this book will ultimately make you laugh and feel good, knowing that you are not alone in experiencing crazy antics at work. I hope that you can relate with the characters as people you know or work with, currently or in the past, and most of all it is my wish that you take away a picture of what good leadership and teamwork looks and feels like. It is my hope that you can then distinguish the difference between what it means to participate versus being committed. And finally, I hope that you can comprehend the monumental success that is achievable when everyone is committed to the goal, to the vision, and most importantly to each other.

When you have managed people for as long as I have, there isn't much you haven't seen or heard, lived through, fought for, or taken a bullet for.

There also isn't much you cannot come up with a fun, creative way to think outside of the box to solve. It's called life experience. Have I made mistakes as a manager? Yes! Have I made bad hiring decisions? Yes! Have I pissed off people along the way? I don't even want to know how many! On the other side of the equation, have I achieved great success? Yes! Have I made awesome hiring decisions? Yes! Have I made co-workers friends for life? Yes! But most importantly, did I do the right things? Treat people fairly? Demonstrate integrity? Put my employees first? Have I changed lives, project outcomes, and companies for the better because of my contributions of time and talent? Emphatically, I believe the answer is "Yes I did!!!"

I am proud of every ring, pin, certificate, trophy, plaque, trip, promotion, or any other acknowledgement I have been awarded in my career. My family still laughs at me because I won't throw them away but keep them stored in a box in the garage. But what I am most proud of is the relationships I have built that have lasted to this day and the trust and respect I built over the years with customers that, if I picked up the phone right now, would still take my call today. I am also proud of the great companies I worked for, the knowledge and training I received, the once in a lifetime career experience I was given to launch a product that changed an industry forever, as well as the privilege of being given the opportunity to make my own career and financial dreams come true.

Last but not least, I was entrusted often with every company's greatest asset: its people. I was given the opportunity to make an impact on their lives, to make them better at their jobs, to teach them to take on more responsibility and act as a team and not just for themselves, while simultaneously always keeping the customer's experience top of mind in every decision. My goal was to instill in everyone that your word is your bond, that it's how you build trust, and that trust is the key to being a huge and consistent success. A Pig's Tale: "Survival is as much a matter of grace as fight" is a tale of how you take where you are, what you've been given, and who you have to do it with, and against all odds you ultimately Make Pig Magic!

TEAMWORK + TRUST = AMAZING SUCCESS

PROLOGUE

It was the first full week of the new year, which meant the first weekend that wasn't a holiday and the last before Grace was to start her new job. On one hand, Grace was relieved that she had finally received a fair offer for the business she was selling after many tumultuous months of significant financial uncertainty, the existential guilt of her decision to move forward with buying the business when her gut and on site training experience had told her not to, followed by the necessary participation in the exposure of the shady business practices that made her case for the abrupt exit because they did not meet her moral code of ethics, coupled with the harsh reality of her mother's impending death, and a very strained siblings relationship caused by a variety of questions and issues relating to her mother's illness and the care Grace was providing, left Grace in a state of acute stress and not at all mentally prepared to step back into a corporate environment or management position of any kind. Grace was understandably fragile, emotionally exhausted, feeling somewhat hopeless and numb, and in desperate need of some rest and self care.

Nonetheless life goes on, a festive weekend was still planned in celebration of the end of the holidays with friends as well as her accomplishment in both selling the business and starting a new job.

On the agenda for Saturday was a full-body deep tissue massage in the afternoon as well as a fancy steak dinner in the evening, followed by a Sunday family day before things started to settle into a new routine.

Grace rarely indulged herself in spa treatments, but it was a holiday gift given to her that she was desperately looking forward to taking full advantage of based on how she was feeling. She hoped it would be fifty minutes of pure bliss that, with every stroke, would release all the tension built up over the last few years since buying the business and her mother's health decline and restore the sense of equanimity and equilibrium she so desperately needed to start this new job.

Now relaxed, showered, dressed, and ready to go, Grace and her husband drove to the restaurant for an evening of laughter, friendship, and great food. After the dinner was completed, the decision was made to end the evening with a nightcap at an establishment next door. As everyone sat chatting and laughing with friends, Grace was overcome with a strong wave of nausea that was undeniably going to end with her becoming sick. Grace abruptly grabbed her husband's hand and stated, "We have to go now, I'm going to be sick." Quick goodbyes were given along with well wishes on the new job, and out the door they went.

Grace barely made it to the safety of her bathroom at home before becoming violently ill for the first of many times that night. Along with the nausea also came body aches, chills, fever, dizziness, and an overwhelming feeling of just how bad this night was going to get. Back and forth to the bathroom Grace went until the early hours of dawn. Finally, Grace lay down exhausted, dehydrated, and almost delirious from her experience of the previous night, and she closed her eyes to finally seek some rest. And that's when Grace began to experience the most vivid, colorful, realistic, and detailed sequence of dreams she had ever experienced in her life.

In her dream, Grace was no longer a female business owner—she was a pig with a flight plan that, if followed, could teach other pigs how to fly. The experience was truly surreal.

When Grace finally awoke late the next morning, all she could think about was her sequence of dreams. She was so consumed by it that her family thought she was still delirious from being so sick, but Grace would not be deterred. She couldn't get her hands on a pen and notepad quick enough to jot down the details of what she experienced. In fact, despite feeling so worn out, Grace insisted on doing some research on the computer to understand what dreams of flying pigs meant. This is what she found.

WHAT DOES IT MEAN WHEN YOU DREAM ABOUT A PIG FLYING?

- If you see a pig flying, it means you will overcome what you thought were insurmountable odds, and challenges will readily fall away, making way for your success in an endeavor.

Even more intrigued by that response, Grace researched the meaning of bizarre dreams and to her relief found that a University of Bern, Switzerland study found that the more bizarre your dream is, the better it is for your brain. The research indicated that realistic but bizarre dreams actually help the brain learn from previous experiences.

Grace, weak and exhausted from the last forty-eight hours of illness and the evening of bizarre dreams, went to bed early Sunday—but not before reviewing her notes and adding to them in even more detail. This experience was something that was so timely, unique, and visceral that Grace knew it would make a great story that one day would need to be shared.

FLYING: THREE STEPS TO GO FROM FEAR TO FUN

1. **Understanding the Fear**

2. **Dealing with the Fear**

3. **Practice and Enjoy**

No one is fearless. Many of us develop a fear of some kind during our lifetime.

Most fears are learned behaviors as opposed to innate. We ask ourselves all kinds of questions focused more on the negative as opposed to the what ifs and possibilities. Are your concerns more about being in control than letting go? Instead of focusing on the worst case, what's the best-case scenario?

Once you know the category your fear falls into, you need to deal with it. Sometimes it's helpful to share your fears with others so they can help you through it. All types of techniques can be learned to help cope with fear. Sometimes just admitting the fear out loud helps to put it into perspective.

Most importantly, own the fear and start taking small steps to conquer it. Create goals for yourself. Surround yourself with people that are successful in overcoming fear. Accept that there will be wins and losses. What doesn't kill you always makes you stronger.

Part One

UNDERSTANDING
THE FEAR

A PIG IN A POKE

The expression "pig in a poke" means an offer or deal that is foolishly accepted without being closely examined first. A poke is a sack or bag.

"If wishes were wings, pigs would fly."

—ROBERT JORDAN

Despite feeling sick as a dog that rainy, chilly January morning after spending the previous Saturday night and all of Sunday in bed with what seemed like a wicked case of "new job" stomach flu, Grace Fully stepped out of her car, pulled her coat tightly around her and walked slowly and unsteadily from the parking lot up the stairs and into the lobby of the building where the first day of her new job was to begin. As soon as she stepped into the building, the contrast of the heat with the damp cold chills she was shaking off sent another wave of nausea over her, much like it had when she had interviewed two months before. Grace could never quite put her finger on it, but something about this place had made her feel apprehensive, and it still did.

Slowly she pushed the elevator button to the third floor, waited, and then stepped out, not knowing what to expect or if she was going to make it through the day.

A short minute later, Grace arrived at the locked, glassed-in wall of the main office, pushed the button to give her name and announce her arrival, and waited for the click that would take her into a world she knew absolutely nothing about. Slowly and cautiously, she walked to the reception area and told the woman sitting there, "This is my first day, and I'm not really sure where I am supposed to go." The receptionist once again asked her name, job title, and the manager she was reporting to, and then asked her to take a seat. Grace was more than willing to sit down; she actually would have preferred to be sent home, as she was worn out just from the trip from the parking lot and was sweating, had chills, and fought back nausea with every fiber of her being.

Just as Grace was starting to feel normal again, a rather large, unfriendly, stalwart looking soul with a scowl on her face called Grace's name and told her to follow her to her desk. She was head of security and needed to take Grace's photograph for her security badge to have access to all the floors in the building. Not one for conversation, when they arrived at her desk she pointed the camera at Grace, clicked it, and said she'd be right back with her badge. When she returned, handing Grace her new badge, Grace glanced down at the photo of herself and wanted to cry. Grace wondered, "Do I really look this rough and miserable?" Before she could think another thought or say thank you, she was being ushered to the Human Resource Department.

Arriving in HR, Grace was again asked to sit in a cubicle, handed a heavy folder of paperwork by another clerk, and left alone to complete the requisite basic new-hire paperwork for taxes, benefits, insurance, blah blah blah…It took over an hour to complete. Grace had questions, but no one appeared to answer them, so she left the spaces blank where she didn't know how to answer and hoped someone would come for her soon. Well, Grace soon learned to be careful what you wish for because at 10:55 a.m. another clerk appeared and told her to move to another space and how lucky she was that her first day was an All Employee Meeting Day.

Upon entering the large conference room, Grace's eyes grew wide at the sight of everyone she would soon be meeting and working with, and she knew for sure all those eyes were looking back at her, the new kid on the block. Just as Grace was about to head to the back corner of the room, the CEO, Petunia Squiggles, tapped her on the shoulder and told her to stay standing in the front of the room as it was tradition to introduce all new employees and have them say a few words about themselves and why they were happy to be there. "I do believe I am going to be sick this minute," thought Grace. Why didn't anybody tell me to come prepared for this? I can barely stand up, I am so sick to my stomach, and now I have to tell everyone why I am happy to be here when the truth is I am anything but happy at this moment.

When Grace's name was spoken, she stepped forward to the X-marked spot on the floor and stated her name, her basic work background, and that she was happy to be there because while she had lots of experience in sales and marketing, she had no experience in the industry of aeronautics, so she was looking forward to learning lots of new things, loved a challenge, and looked forward to working closely with all her fellow employees in the room. It was like an out- of-body experience where some other person's voice was coming out of Grace's mouth. What she wanted to say was, "I feel so sick right now, so can I please just go home?" but nooooooo, this competitive voice took right over, said all the right things, gained applause and was finally rewarded with a chair to sit down in for the rest of the two-hour meeting.

After the meeting adjourned, one of Grace's new direct reports, Babe, offered to show her to the second floor where the team sat and help her get her cubicle set up. Grace accepted the kind offer and followed her into the elevator and down to the second floor. Babe let Grace try out her new badge at the door to make sure it worked, upon entering, walked three feet and said, "Okay, this is your space." Maybe it was because of how bad Grace was feeling since she had arrived at 9 a.m. and it was now 1 p.m. and her last meal had been eaten Saturday night before she got sick or because she was wondering if this was some kind of cruel new-hire initiation trick, but the space she was led to was so pitiful that Grace just stood there with her mouth agape with incredulity. It wasn't that it was your run-of-the-mill padded cubicle—this particular space was more like a triangle than a cube, in that it only had three sides to it and where the opening to enter was a floor to ceiling four-foot-thick pole blocking the entry. To make matters worse, it was right by the door she had just come in through, so the sound of the door opening and closing would be heard all day. Since no one had ever been put in that space before, it had become everyone's shortcut around the pole to the exit. All things considered—constant noise, traffic, no privacy, the pole, and only three sides to the cube—it reminded Grace more of her very own personal Bermuda Triangle. You know, that place where aircraft and ships are often said to have disappeared under mysterious circumstances.

Babe stayed around for a bit, helping Grace get her computer set up and logged in and showing her where to find the basics like e-mail, expenses, the outline of courses she needed to take to get trained in what was done there, and all the product information she would need to know. She then took her on a brief tour, re-introducing the team she was now responsible to manage in this office and where they sat and showing her who her closest neighbors were, their names, and what they did. Then she left her alone to take it all in, process, and decide for herself, "Should I stay or just make a run for it?"

After about an hour, the basic introduction to aeronautics course was completed, and Grace was giving serious consideration to what she should tackle next. Finally, she got up from her desk, walked over to Babe, explained how sick she had been all weekend, and said she realized that it was only 3 p.m. but that at this point she felt so weak, tired, and nauseous that she had to leave early and go home. (Much later on, Babe told her the team members took bets as to whether she would actually return the next day. Surprisingly to all, but most of all to Grace, they all lost!)

After a long night's rest and a little food in her stomach, Grace somehow managed to wake up feeling better physically, shower, get dressed, and head back in for day two on the new job. That day the agenda included more online training courses, a managers meeting, and a sit-down meeting with her new boss, R. E. Pigglesworth, the Vice President of

Sales. Grace had liked R.E. when she'd interviewed with him several months back. He had been open and gracious enough to take a chance on an outsider with no specific experience in aeronautics but who had worked in many related fields that could bring a fresh perspective on challenges and projects. But the main reason he had chosen Grace was because of the number and variety of teams she had managed in her career—and all with great success stories to tell. Grace recalled him calling it something like "making magic wherever she went."

After settling in her triangular cube, Grace walked around and greeted her team members, who looked both surprised and bummed at the same time because their new boss actually did come back for a Day Two. She also completed another online training course before heading upstairs to the managers meeting. The next two hours were filled with discussions about opportunities, issues, challenges, what was working and what wasn't. All the while, Grace sat listening but neither contributing nor comprehending one word of what was being said. Between the high-level details of aeronautics which Grace did not yet comprehend and the in-house acronyms for all the projects, Grace felt as if the meeting was being held in some meeting room in another country, in another language, in another place in time. It was hard to stay focused and look interested. Finally, lunch was brought in and the formal meeting adjourned, but everyone hung out to eat and chat. Next up was Grace's meeting with her new boss.

Grace was nervous and still not feeling completely well, so she ate very little and then ran to the ladies' room to freshen up and calm her nerves before the meeting. Everyone was gone when she returned except R.E., who asked her to have a seat so the meeting could begin.

After a few minutes of general chit chat, R.E. began the meeting by telling Grace why she was there, a little about her team, and what his expectations of her would be for the first six months. He once again, as he had done in the interview process, reassured Grace that while she was brought in as a Manager, he was confident because of her past successes, vast experience, and previous job titles that he would be able to increase her salary and get her promoted in six months to a Director. R.E. knew this was important to Grace because she had hesitated to accept the position when it was offered. That part covered, Grace said "Tell me about my team."

It was now R.E. 's turn to look a bit uncomfortable when he began speaking, until he finally admitted that he himself had just inherited Grace's team under him in the New Year, and he knew absolutely nothing about them that would help her. All he could share was that, anecdotally, the impression that had been formed around the company was that no one really knew what they did, who they did it for, or how they got it done. They had built a reputation as being unreliable, lazy, and some even combative in nature. No one knew whether they were sales or service in their job description, and what he needed Grace to do most was rein them in and figure out what they did all day. "Hmmm," said Grace, "that wasn't the picture that you painted for me in November when I interviewed, R.E. In fact, you allowed them to interview me as part of the process of getting the job. Why would you do that if this is the real situation?" R. E. squirmed some more in his chair and said, "Because I don't know what to do with them or for them, so I thought they should at least get a vote in who their new boss would be before he or she decided what their futures would look like."

Grace sighed deeply, once again feeling a wave of discomfort and nausea with the whole prospect of being in this position. Finally, Grace looked at R.E. straight in the eye and asked him directly, "What would you do if you were me in this position?" He didn't hesitate for a second to respond with, "Based on what I've heard anecdotally, if I were you, I'd fire them all and start all over again." Grace was taken aback. "Wow...I wasn't expecting that response. So,why didn't you mention this little situation when I interviewed in November?" R.E. responded, "Because then I knew you wouldn't come, and I needed someone that could help me fix this conundrum. I needed someone who could evaluate the situation, develop a course of action, implement it, and weed out the good from the bad while I focused on the sales and growth part of the business." Silence ensued between them for what felt like eternity, until Grace finally spoke up and said, "Give me six months to assess the situation, let me do things my way, and at the end of that time period, we will review my progress and accomplishments and then discuss in more detail what my future, career, title, and job scope will look like. Do we have a deal?" "Yes, we do," said Mr. Pigglesworth.

Damn, there went that power mouth again! Two times in two days!

READER PARTICIPATION & REFLECTION EXERCISES

I typically find that at the end of a chapter of any book I read, there are unanswered questions or thoughts that went through my mind as I was reading it that I want to make sure I capture. I really want to keep the story straight, keep track of the characters introduced, understand their roles clearly, and truly immerse myself in what the characters are feeling at that point. It helps me relate better to what is happening in the story and separates facts from feelings. It also may help you relate what you might be experiencing in your life to one of the characters or situations in the book.

Depending on your own learning style, you may like to write your responses into this book, say them out loud, or simply reflect on them silently.

CHAPTER 1 LESSON: TRUST YOUR GUT! THINGS AREN'T ALWAYS WHAT THEY SEEM

1. What is the actual "pig in a poke" of this chapter?

2. What are the Six Ground Rules of Leadership?

3. If you were Grace, how would you handle the situation she was just placed in?

4. What are the "pig in a poke" situations you've been placed in? How did you handle them?

5. Why do you think R.E. Pigglesworth chose Grace Fully over other candidates when members of the team she would be managing didn't want her due to her lack of specific industry experience?

LIPSTICK ON A PIG

To "put lipstick on a pig" is a rhetorical expression used to convey the message that making superficial or cosmetic changes is a futile attempt to disguise the true nature of a product.

> *"You can't solve problems by using the same kind of thinking we used when we created them."*

— ALBERT EINSTEIN

When Grace got back to work on Wednesday, she was still somewhat in shock from what the first two days on the job had revealed. It really does go to show that those gut instincts that said something just didn't feel right when she interviewed in November and made her initially stall her job acceptance and then her start day until January were dead on. The million-dollar question for her was, "What do I do about it now?"

Grace arrived at her cubicle, logged in, and went around and greeted her team with a cheery good morning. "Maybe I can win them over initially with kindness, punctuality, and assuring them that I am there for them. It's as good a place to start as any," she thought. But Grace scheduled time in between getting herself up to speed with product knowledge modules on the training portal to draft out a ninety-day plan to attack the challenges she faced.

With a notebook and pen in hand, Grace moved away from her cubicle and found a small office to quiet her environment and focus her mind on the ninety-day plan. While Grace knew she was an experienced and successful manager, all of her past successes had come in environments where she had also been a product expert. She shivered when she reminded herself of the previous day's team meeting where she had sat for hours not understanding anything about what they were talking about.

In her notebook, Grace wrote at the top of the page: "My Ninety-Day Plan to a Winning Team." After staring at the blank page for what seemed like hours, Grace began to scribble her ideas and thoughts. She began by numbering the ideas 1-5 in order of the priority in which they had to happen so that the success and momentum could build on itself. If this workplace loved its acronyms as much as it had seemed they did in that meeting, surely she could come up with a few of her own to fit in and accomplish what needed to get done in her first ninety days. The following was her first effort:

E M P T E

1. **Evaluate** the players by setting up one-on-one's. Have them individually explain their roles, their internal and external customers, and what they think are the greatest areas of opportunity/challenges that they face daily. Try to meet their families and have lunch or dinner. Through that experience, try to gain a better understanding of what their job entails, who their customers are, what the challenges and obstacles to their success are, and personally understand their motivations, priorities, dreams for their careers, and specific family needs.

2. **Meet** the internal strategic partners we interact with and service to determine where we are meeting expectations, timelines, and quality of work standards or not. How could we help more?

3. **Put heads together** with the managers of other departments to get their input on individuals and the team as a whole. What are their impressions? What do they see as our role? Who do they think is performing well or under-performing? Get their opinion on what they could do better. Find out what they are doing to be successful.

4. **Tally** collected and analyzed data. Encapsulate the findings and report back to the team what they are, and then lay out the course for the future. Describe in great detail the what, where, why, when, and how for accomplishing our goals.

5. **Expose** more about yourself, your style, your goals, your fears, your strengths and weaknesses. Paint your vision of what success would look like and how would we know when we achieved it. Read the individual reactions to this information and determine who is on board.

It took several hours to complete that list, but Grace felt good that she, at least on paper, was on the right path. How others would respond to her style and approach would bring about its own new set of challenges—of that she was certain. Grace went back to her cubicle and immediately began scheduling ninety-minute meetings with her team members, and she made flight arrangements to meet the folks in the other office location.

THE HOME OFFICE TEAM/HOG JAW

BABE

Grace's first impression of Babe was a positive one. She seemed young, ambitious, confident, smart, and capable of articulating on a level such that a newcomer like Grace could understand what her role was, yet she could also speak the corporate language that was still so foreign to Grace. She took the ninety minutes seriously, came prepared, talked about her customers, and explained that she felt her role was both sales and service and could cite examples of both. She went into detail about the history of the team, the previous manager, and how no one really knew or valued what they did. She offered her opinion on her teammates, the challenges they faced, the perceptions and misperceptions others had of them and why. She talked about her husband, where she went to school, how long she had worked there, what she liked about the company, and who to watch out for. She and Grace ended their time together laughing about how sick Grace had looked on day one and how unsure she had been that Grace would even come back for day two. So far, she was happy that she had. Babe demonstrated both candor and courage, two qualities that Grace valued very, very much.

Grace promptly placed her in the keeper column. Next up was Elvis.

ELVIS

Grace's visit with Elvis was in direct contrast to the one the day before with Babe. Grace's impression thus far of him had been that he was handsome, popular, funny, engaging, and well connected with other employees and top leadership, but she had also heard he had a bad habit of disappearing or calling in sick due to excruciating body pain that required frequent treatments of some sort. Elvis did not look at all happy to spend the next ninety minutes with Grace. He talked a lot more about who he knew, who he was tight with, how he was one of the original members of the company, and how he and the president hung out at conventions and such, yet he was more evasive around questions like how he spent his days or how he prioritized his work, who his customers were, and what their greatest needs were. He also focused a lot on telling Grace about how the company had a great work-from-home policy and that he would like to keep taking advantage of it. Grace couldn't quite put her finger on the vibe she was getting from Elvis other than to conclude that something just wasn't quite on the up and up with him—and perhaps that he was hiding something.

Grace put Elvis on the no/must watch closer list.

SPAMALA

Finally, Grace got to spend time with Spamala. Spamala wasn't much more tenured at the company than Grace, but she had been around at least three months because Grace remembered her from the interview. Spamala was closer in age to Grace than either Babe or Elvis, and she had many years of direct industry experience. Grace felt that Spamala could be a tremendous team asset to build on for others less experienced, as well as an outlet for Grace to ask questions if she was willing to gain her trust. It was obvious that Spamala knew the business, but Grace was feeling a bit of Spam's skepticism and a very real reluctance to open up completely. Grace could somewhat relate to that with this job not being her first rodeo, so it was important to Grace to work on establishing respect and trust with Spamala, to get her to be more of a team player, and to encourage her to be open to share her wealth of experience with others. Spamala had high energy and enthusiasm levels and a sarcastic wit that made everyone laugh, and she was known for some of her clever "isms" like her parting advice at the meeting: "Lay low, keep direct deposit, and don't get too intimate with your sh** at work." While it was witty, Grace wasn't quite sure what to make of the underlying meaning of her message about herself and the company.

Grace put Spamala on the maybe list. She had high hopes to win her over but needed to establish ground rules and mutual respect.

Grace was only halfway through her team evaluations and was scheduled to go to the western home office the next week to complete the balance, but when she got back to her cubicle, she wrote down her honest assessment of this portion of her team as one yes, one no, one maybe. Disillusioned by her findings, Grace began to play with her computer, looking desperately for something to spark an idea—a mascot, a story, a theme—anything that would help her right this capsizing ship.

Grace must have researched a hundred different concepts and fallen into a daydream because the next thing she remembered, she was blushing and stuttering, trying to explain to Elvis, as he stood in her cube, why there were pictures of pigs, piggy banks, and piglets plastered all over her screen. "I am looking for a symbol of inspiration to build this team around," she explained as he walked away laughing and thinking his new boss, as he'd suspected, was some kind of kook and wouldn't last very long, just as the many others before her hadn't.

It was that day that Grace decided to call upon a friend who was a full-time employee there but also a public traffic/safety officer part time to get a few yards of the bright yellow crime scene tape to hang as a joke for her team as well as a deterrent to other would-be intruders who tried to cut through her cube to avoid the four-foot floor to ceiling pole.

The crime scene tape wrapped around Grace's cube and the pole stopped everyone in their tracks, and it brought much laughter and conversation to all who passed. Grace hoped it was also expressing to her co-workers her playful and open-hearted nature.

> **See Ground Rule #1:** Stay true to who you are, in the six ground rules of leadership. Meaning Grace wanted to act in ways that aligned with her own values and feelings rather than conforming to the values and feelings she was currently picking up from her team, her peers, and her leadership. Grace was well aware of her strengths and weaknesses in this situation, and was very open and honest with herself about the immediate limitations she had, but, she understood boundaries needed to be set and was looking for team building activities and relationships that would make all their job performance and satisfaction much better

THE HOME OFFICE TEAM/HOG DAWG

After an early morning wake-up call, a long drive to the airport, and a flight halfway across the country, Grace landed in the big Hog D. She had arranged to have a driver pick her up at the airport and transport her to the other home office. From the office chatter, thus far Grace had gleaned that the employees that worked in this location considered themselves to be the ugly and forgotten red-headed stepchildren of the main office in Hog J. No senior management person worked or managed out of this location every day, so things were run a little looser there.

Communication was sometimes received, sometimes not. Teamwork with the other location was challenging at best to non-existent at worst. One stop at the security desk and a short elevator ride later, and Grace landed at her destination. On her agenda today was meeting Guinea, Barbie, and Ava. After being allowed in and shown her space to use for the next two days by the very kind and thoughtful receptionist, Grace went over to meet her team and begin to take in the atmosphere and vibe of this second location. After a casual conversation with the team over a cup of coffee in the break room to shake off the jet lag, Grace got to work by meeting with Gwin.

GUINEA (GWIN)

Gwin and Grace got off to a great start. While intimidating to Grace in her physically fit presence, Gwin had a very kind heart, was incredibly smart, was an introvert like herself, and lacked the self-confidence to know how good she truly was at her job. No one else on the team did the specific line of work that she did, so Grace began to see two glaring challenges right away in bringing the team together. The first challenge was the distance/separation, and the second was that the six team members performed three entirely different job functions but were bunched together as one group. Grace was overwhelmed at the thought of learning three distinctly different job functions and all the nuances associated with each, but she put those thoughts aside and chose to make her work about the people, not the specifics of each job.

Gwin was a single mom with three children, so she needed this job and worked very hard at it. Like Babe in the other office, she was prepared and told Grace everything about what she did, the subtleties of that office, and the challenges she faced—and did so with such a command of knowledge and confidence. Grace, of course, had no idea what she was talking about, but at that point, she was looking for body language, style, strengths, weaknesses, and confidence. She also wanted to see if there was an opportunity to build trust with her and determine if she was a leader or follower. In a lot of ways, Grace and Gwin were alike, introverts but confident in their abilities.

Grace quickly put her on the yes/keeper list.

BARBIE

In contrast, Barbie and Grace did not mesh well. Barbie was a lot like Elvis in that she knew everybody, and everybody knew Barbie. Grace had heard that Barbie was often confrontational and that the previous manager had tried to fire Barbie but in the end couldn't get it done because she was afraid of Barbie. Again, no one else knew what she did or how she did it. Barbie was also in the same age range as Grace and was very talkative about all the customers who loved her so much and couldn't live without her. She talked about how the company just couldn't function without her either, but when asked to describe her day, her goals, and how she managed her work, her response was, "Everything is a fire drill here, so it can't be managed. I just take good care of my customers." Ninety minutes with Barbie seemed like a lifetime. Her style of communication was, in a word, intimidating. Grace felt Barbie was hiding something and that she did a lot of talking, there was no way to measure her results, so Grace cut it short to get to the final team member, who was also very new to the company.

Grace put Barbie on a no/must watch closer list—something was not right.

AVA

Last but not least, there was Ava. Ava had been hired right before Grace for the purpose of helping Barbie, who had complained that there was so much work to be done, and she just couldn't do it all. The reality was that Barbie was supposed to be training Ava on her part of the business, splitting up her accounts with her so that together they would both be able to get more business. So, the obvious question Grace had to ask was "How is that working out so far?"

Ava was an attractive, polished professional, well spoken, intelligent, and confident in her abilities. She didn't know Grace or what the future held, so she carefully chose her words in response to the questions. It appeared that Ava and Gwin were building a relationship and working well together, but it was a bit more of a struggle with Barbie. As Ava carefully chose her words, it became clear that it had been somewhat of a challenge to get Barbie to sit down to explain and review each customer's status. Barbie was also reluctant to split up the customers (which was the main reason why Ava was hired) because they all loved her so much and she was afraid Ava wasn't up to the task. Barbie, however, wasn't training Ava or communicating with her what the actual tasks were. So Grace pointedly asked Ava, "So you've been here almost two months with little to no work to do, no training, and no guidance—is that a fair assessment to date?" Ava responded "Yes," affirming that nothing productive had happened other than the self- initiative she had taken to meet with other employees, understand their roles, and spend as much time with Gwin as possible to learn what she could from her. With her background of achievements, it was easy to see the frustration already building for Ava. Grace thanked her for her time, stated that she was working on a ninety-day plan to get this team going in the right direction, and asked for her patience and trust because with every passing day the picture was becoming clearer as to what needed to be done.

Grace put Ava on the maybe list and knew engaging her more was needed to keep her.

So there it was. The results of the second team weren't much different than the first team: one yes, one no, one maybe. In summary, the two offices were two yeses, two nos, and two maybes. While the results were glum to say the least, there was still more hope than what R.E. had suggested initially.

Grace continued down her list of the Top Five tasks that needed to be done in ninety days by meeting with key Strategic Partners, and she took time with other department managers to get their feedback on the team as a whole. Grace asked about individual experiences with team members, looking for honest and open feedback and specific examples that were good or not so good. One of the biggest takeaways for Grace, though, and one that was much more troubling than her own team issues, was a deeply enrooted, almost endemic in the culture of the company, sense or perception that no one really felt that anyone cared about them as individuals, regardless of their job. The culture was made up of the haves and have nots. No one was to be trusted entirely. People mysteriously disappeared if they challenged the status quo: "Poof" was the descriptive word used most often. Accountability was optional. "Just say no, it can't be done" was the commonplace theme. And finally, no one felt a sense of belonging to a community that cared about what they did or knew if what they were doing made a difference. It seemed like everyone was just working to make a paycheck and saving themselves to fight another day.

It became abundantly clear that the issues and challenges her department faced mirrored those of the whole company, especially when, after interviewing or meeting with all these key business partners, Grace was barraged with responses like "Why are you doing this? Nobody cares," or "You are not like anyone we have ever had here before." She was also asked, "What's your endgame here?" and told, "Nothing here ever changes" or "You better watch your back and your front because no one challenges the status quo here." And finally from Spamala: "You can save the world or Free Willy, but you can't do both!"

Grace was not necessarily shocked by these comments after being there sixty days, but she knew she wasn't ready to take on the whole world. She did feel confident that she was now armed with enough ammunition to set a course for her own team's survival.

Grace made the executive decision that it was time to bring the team together in Hog Jaw to communicate her findings, lay out what her vision of success would look like for the team, and, above all, make the meeting about her people. That meant she would take steps to begin to build trust with and among them, encourage honesty and accountability, and most of all let them know that they now had someone on their team that had their back.

READER PARTICIPATION & REFLECTION EXERCISES

"You can put lipstick and earrings on a hog and call her Monique, but it's still a pig."

—ANN RICHARDS

CHAPTER 2 LESSON: YOU CAN TRY & DRESS SOMETHING UP, BUT IT IS WHAT IT IS

1. The phrase "put lipstick on a pig" means making superficial changes or cosmetic changes to a product in a futile effort to disguise its failings. What specifically were the top three things that were failing on this team?

2. EMPTE stood for **E**valuate, **M**eet strategic partners, **P**ut heads together with managers of different teams to discover what was working for them, **T**ally the feedback, and **E**xpose to the team who Grace was, what she was thinking, and the direction she was planning for the team. What is the value to the manager/team of this process?

3. In meeting one-on-one with each team member, what were the messages Grace was sending out to her team? What messages were the team members sending back to Grace?

4. What role did the feedback from Grace's peers on her team and the company culture in general have in firming up the strategy she decided to move forward with?

5. Given this set of circumstances to work with as a manager, what would you do and why?

THE THREE LITTLE PIGS

"Who lives in a house like this?"

—THE BIG BAD WOLF

"People want guidance not rhetoric. They need to know what the plan of action is and how it will be implemented. They want to be given responsibility to help solve the problem and authority to take action on it."

—HOWARD SCHULZ

The Three Little Pigs is a fable about three pigs who are sent out into the world by their mother to seek their fortune. The pigs were family but took two distinctly different attitudes toward life. The first two focused on play and instant gratification while the third was able to postpone play to do what was right. He planned strategically and worked hard to build a solid foundation. Each pig would go on to build their house of a different material: straw, sticks, or bricks. Only one house, however, ultimately survived the big bad wolf—the one made with bricks! Because of his role model behavior of empathy, deliberation, and understanding, the pig who built this house was also able to save his two brothers. Hard work and dedication pays off!

What are you building your house with? That is the very question Grace was about to put before her team and use as a metaphor to manage this team moving forward.

The day finally arrived for Grace to hold her first team meeting. As experienced as Grace was, she couldn't help but feel a bit of anxiety as the newest member of the team, with no experience in the industry. Also, now knowing the players even just a little bit, she knew how indifferently they might react to her style of management. Was she just another talking head, or was she the real deal? Additionally, Grace had learned that departments at her new company did not typically hold team meetings, fly employees from one office to the other, or even plan or do any team building activities, so she was in unchartered territory, and wasn't even sure she wasn't breaking any rules or if she had the budget to do what she was about to do. Grace just knew that open communication and dialogue was critical if she was to show signs of success in the six- month timeframe she had given to her boss. At this point, Grace was already ninety days into the job and wasn't exactly observing much job satisfaction, inclusiveness, or passion from the people she worked with, so she felt she had nothing to lose and oh so much to gain.

One observation Grace had made in her first ninety days was that there was almost this sense of a "mean girls club," like back in high school where she was the outsider until proven to be worthy of being included and God forbid that she would try to make herself stand out in any positive way. One encounter in an elevator with a female VP began with a brief verbal exchange that went something like, "Just who do you think you are, and what exactly are you trying to prove? You look the part, dress the part, and have the pedigree to play—you just won't! Why? We are watching you!" The elevator door opened, and the VP stepped out before Grace had time to respond. The message, however, had been delivered loud and clear. People were indeed watching, the culture of the company was set, and Grace was not following the unwritten rules. Today's team meeting was about to rock their world as they knew it.

THE MEETING

Everyone cautiously gathered around the table to find a seat for the team meeting that would forever change their lives. Not knowing what to expect, the team members exchanged nervous giggles and glances, and perhaps a few even may have rolled their eyes, but Grace was not to be discouraged or derailed from her mission.

Grace proudly took her place at the head of the table and kicked off the meeting by welcoming everyone, reviewing the agenda, and stating that the goal of the meeting was to begin to establish a relationship of trust with her, each other, their partners, and the customers they served. She went on to explain that with real trust anything was possible, and without it they were doomed to failure as individuals and as a team. Trust was a word that everyone used freely, but without truly experiencing trust at a level they had never experienced before, they could neither comprehend its meaning nor its power.

> _**Trust** (noun): assured reliance on the character, ability, strength or truth of someone or something._
>
> **—MERRIAM-WEBSTER**

Grace continued by explaining that there were actually two types of trust: practical and emotional. Practical trust was basic. Be hard working, show up on time, and do what you say you'll do when you say you'll do it. Emotional trust was a lot more difficult to achieve. It required having each other's backs, feeling comfortable sharing ideas and feelings, and respecting each other's knowledge, abilities, strengths, and weaknesses. Grace's plan for this meeting and moving forward was to build both types.

Grace then explained that they would be participating in an exercise that would not only initiate trust within their group but would push their comfort zone in front of their peers. Grace passed around a sheet of paper that had several topics people could choose as prompts to talk about themselves and share with the group: some things they didn't know about each other and some that they might. If a team was going to emerge from this group, vulnerability would have to go first to foster closeness and intimacy, and Grace as the leader would have to let them know who she truly was, how she thought, what she valued, and what she aspired to do, so Grace volunteered to speak first.

My name is Grace Fully. I've been happily married for over twenty-one years, and I have two children, a daughter and a son. In addition to this job and raising my children, I am sole caretaker of my parents in my home, both of whom are suffering and declining with issues related to cancer. To be perfectly honest with you, I am not sure this is the right job for me. I took this position because I am in the process of selling my own business. I believe I have a buyer and will close the sale later this year. Owning a business and working in this training/mentoring field the last couple of years, coupled with my vast sales experience, where my job has always been to inspire myself, my peers, my direct reports, and my clients to reach their greatest potential and then keep reaching for even more, seems in direct contrast to what I see being done here. I'm a bit confused in this environment where emotional intelligence, risk taking, and ambition for greatness seem to be discouraged, even punishable by firing if I am to believe everything I've heard. Am I on track here with what I've picked up so far?

Additionally, I am really having a hard time grasping exactly what it is we do here, and no one seems to be eager or willing to help me learn, so if it sometimes seems I'm struggling trying to understand what you are saying or doing, I am. That scares me to death because I have always been an expert in my field, so I feel exceptionally vulnerable to attack by others. What I need most from this group is to identify what each of your areas of expertise is, so you can help me learn, so I in turn can help you be better in your area and protect you from those who wish to do you harm.

What I bring to the table is a wealth of sales and marketing experience, a tremendous track record of success building and growing teams, a fearless management style when it comes to my people, and a commitment to making a difference in the lives of the people I manage and the place where I work. I am not like any other manager you've had or ever will have again. In a nutshell, as a Certified Executive Trainer, I've been taught how to enhance the leadership skills and functioning of motivated, achievement-oriented professionals looking to excel in their current or potential job roles. Simply said, my job is to cultivate more intelligent, aware, and ambitious employees. Are you those people? From everything I've seen and heard these first ninety days, I'm not sure you are. Therefore, I suspect you'll either really like and respect me, knowing I have your best interests at heart and that I am willing to take a bullet for you, or you will fear me because I will expect the same from you in return for me and your teammates.

Know that I know BS when I hear it, and it will not be tolerated. Your word is your bond, and if when you speak people can't believe you or trust you, then you have no credibility or place on this team.

That's a lot to ask, but I also promise that we will have fun, be successful, and also be the team everyone else wants to be on by the time I'm done.

One more thing: family is very important to me, so I will want to know about yours or whatever else is most important to you. My end game is not my own success but helping you to be successful achieving your career dreams and goals. If I do that well, then success for me will follow. Does anyone have any questions or comments on what I've communicated so far?

> **See Ground Rules 1, 2, &4** in the six ground rules of leadership above: Stay true to who you are, practice what you preach, and stand up and show your strength, fortitude, and courage. It was a pedagogical play for Grace to demonstrate her vulnerabilities, share her personal situation, and speak so candidly about her own opinion of the current state of affairs at work, and trust that the team would see the courage or emotional power Grace was demonstrating and the ability to still withstand

more adversity and do the right thing in spite of the consequences, and trust that her team run wouldn't immediately run to management and repeat everything she said and demand a new boss.

Silence filled the room and weighed on everyone like a lead balloon, especially when Grace asked, "So who wants to go next?"

One by one, Grace went around the room asking everyone to share what they felt most comfortable sharing and at least one thing they didn't feel comfortable sharing. She heard about her team's families, past jobs, horror stories of previous managers, more on the company's "poof factor," their perceptions of her, and how they felt no one understood or valued them for the work they did, which left them fearing for their jobs. They also shared the insider secrets of how things really worked, who were the players to be trusted, and others to stay away from. Grace also learned that someone on her team could not swim and was deathly afraid of water, and finally they also fessed up that they had been pretty sure she wouldn't make it to day two.

Everyone had a good laugh over that. It was both a physically and emotionally exhausting exercise, but by the end, it felt like the elephant had at least gone to sit in the corner of the room if not leave it completely, at least for the time being.

After a short break, Grace came back, thanked everyone for their participation and candidness, and then went about sharing all the data she had gathered from her meetings and one-on-ones, the conclusions she had made, and the game plan she was suggesting they needed to follow for the next ninety days. But she also wanted their input and feedback on her learning and their feelings on the comments made by others about them and the observations she and others had made before the plan was put into effect.

In a nutshell, Grace explained that there were five things that consistently came up as issues for the team, and those issues were hurting both individuals' and the team's reputation and credibility, basically leading to what she called a "PR crisis." Grace had decided the strategy was to launch a new PR campaign backed by success stories, visibility, and a symbol of unity, while at the same time creating some buzz around the changes on the team and ultimately adding some fun on the job.

The key problems identified were:

1. No one knew what role the team played and how it benefited the organization.

2. People were taking advantage of the work from home policy, so it appeared that the team was not working.

3. Some individuals on the team were viewed by their own team members and others as not being team players.

4. The work products being delivered were sloppy, late, incorrect, or not what was needed.

5. The team was thought to be lazy and unreliable, and therefore it had no value and could not be trusted.

Grace summed up what she had learned over the last ninety days about her team as a major public relations catastrophe. Their team in the scope of the overall company was a disaster, and she was the only relief resource being sent in to fix or disband the problem.

Grace went on to explain that she did not have all the answers or solutions to their current dilemma, and she also highlighted that she was at a distinct disadvantage in fixing it because of her lack of expertise in aeronautics. To have any chance at succeeding, she needed each and every one of them to be her eyes and ears to what was going on and her product experts as she so delicately maneuvered the political landmines being laid to blow them apart.

So there it was, out in the open, for all participants to absorb and process the monumental challenges they faced as a team. Grace asked each one of them to think about what they learned that day about themselves, their leader, and their teammates and decide if they were all in or out. If they were in, it was going to take a lot of hard work, teamwork, and continued honesty and courage. It wasn't going to be easy, but Grace assured them of two things. First, that no one cared more about them than she did and second, that no one would fight harder for them, assuming they were all in like she was.

> **See Ground Rules 3 & 6**: Love your team and be willing to take a bullet for them to earn their trust. No one at that meeting could deny the deep interest, bond, and commitment Grace was demonstrating to her team. Without knowing all that she needed to know about the business, and all the rules she might be breaking, having this kind of meeting, Grace was willing to dive into unchartered territory and clear a new path to a fresh start for them all.

Grace ended that first half-day of the meeting in a very unorthodox manner, which again shocked and bewildered her team but set the tone and the foundation on which their future success would be built.

She told the team that their team motto would be **P.I.G** and that stood for: **Persistence, Integrity, and Guts,** and that these are the ingredients she deemed necessary for their success.

Then she reached into her briefcase and pulled out a copy of the fable "The Three Little Pigs" and read it to her team. She could only imagine what thoughts were running through their minds as she read them the story, but it was, she felt, the best analogy of how things would be run in her department from that point forward. She felt they were in fact building their own houses, both as individuals and as a team collectively, and one day when the wolf came knocking, who would be ready to withstand the hungry and ambitious wolf?

How you built your house—your reputation, work product, image, problem solving, relationships with others, etc.—would depend on trust and the quality of time, effort, and materials you were going to use to build it. Everybody knows which pig won and beat the fox. Hard work and dedication would pay off. Which one would they choose to be?

Finally, Grace handed out large, brightly colored, ceramic piggy banks and instructed the team to place them prominently on their desks as a reminder of this day. She also instituted an incentive program that would allow each team member or anyone in the company to award someone a "trust fund dollar" for a job well done, being on time, going above and beyond, or to acknowledge a major accomplishment. Whoever earned the most dollars at the end of every month would trade those in for a gift card of their choice.

Just the picture of everyone leaving the meeting carrying pink, blue, crowned, spotted, and otherwise sparkling and colorful piggy banks back to their desks past other employees started the positive buzz and excitement that something big was happening on their team. Grace smiled a huge smile of contentment that for the first time in ninety days, she felt she had her team encouraged and engaged. The foundation was laid, the plan of action was formed, and there were no more excuses or blame, just solutions and ownership. And most importantly. they were empowered to control their own destiny.

See Ground Rule 3: Love your Team! — Enough Said!

FIVE FOUNDATIONS TO SUCCESS

1. Strategic guidance, not rhetoric

2. Deliberate plan of action

3. Responsibility to solve problems

4. Empowerment to take ownership and action

5. A manager that is committed to their success

FIVE FOUNDATIONS TO SUCCESS

The key to success is yours, if you can count to five
Provide clear direction and not some juke and jive
Follow that direction with a class of instruction
And watch with awe at the increase in production
Take ownership of problems that need to be solved
And watch lifetime observers begin to get involved
Empower them with authority to take immediate action
And the seeds of confidence will take root and gain traction
Be a leader committed to the success of your team
Achieve amazing results and watch them live their dream

— GRACE FULLY

READER PARTICIPATION & REFLECTION EXERCISES

CHAPTER 3 LESSON: YOUR WORD IS YOUR BOND. IT'S HOW YOU BUILD A STRONG HOUSE

1. In this chapter, Grace's vulnerability, honesty, and challenges she faced personally and professionally were presented for the whole team to see. What do you think she was trying to accomplish by doing this with her team?

2. What do you think Grace's team's perception of her was at this point: strength or weakness? How do you think the team would respond to her from that point on?

3. How do the Five Foundations to Success mirror what happened in that first team meeting?

4. Why do you think Grace chose the story of "The Three Little Pigs" to emphasize exactly where the team was at that point in time? What impressions did she make with her team by reading it to them?

5. What impact did giving everyone a piggy bank to place in their cubicles have on the mindset of her team as well as the other people that worked there?

Part Two

DEALING WITH THE FEAR

MAKE PIG MAGIC!

Magic (noun): the power of apparently influencing the course of events by using mysterious or supernatural forces.

—MERRIAM-WEBSTER.COM

"If you've gotten yourself into a pickle by being a hotdog, perhaps you haven't peeled your own onion.! Go within; relish the silence and ketchup with your true self."

—DAVID ROPPO

Grace was now fully engaged in the next phase of building her team. With the timeline she had given R.E.at their first meeting, the next ninety days were critical to establishing with confidence that her team was viable, committed to making positive contributions to the company and thereby worthy of saving their jobs.

Grace planned her monthly calendar so that she could split her time between both offices to become more ingrained culturally in how the teams worked in both locations and to help create a culture of confidence and reliability of the team members on each other. As projects came up, Grace paired team members together from both locations so that they could learn more about what each other did and how they could be more effective at maintaining business, selling additional services, and settling client conflicts by having a go-to person for each scenario. Grace also made the decision to appoint one person in each location to be the Team Lead over the other team members so that in her absence there would be order, consistency, and authority over accountability on deliverables.

For the most part, things were going better than expected. The piggy banks were a huge morale booster and a great incentive to do things right the first time between the team and with the internal and external customers we served. Everyone in the offices wanted their own piggy bank!

Often, when things got rough, or if the team did an excellent job, Grace would take the team members out for a mid-afternoon ice cream break. Grace believed every problem could be solved over a scoop of vanilla ice cream. Because of that tradition, Grace gave each team member a biker pig ice cream scoop that she had found somewhere in her travels as a symbol of the tradition and a way to carry the spirit of their new-found unity home with them.

However, there were still concerns that weighed heavily on Grace's mind and heart. They were all people-related. First, she had no clear direction from her manager (R.E.) or any feedback from him that what she was doing was good or bad, on track or not, or what he even envisioned for the team in the broader scope. And she also knew that one employee in each location needed to be let go but wasn't sure if she had his support or what the documentation process was in this company. Grace decided it was time for a midterm check-up with her boss.

MIDTERM MEETING

Overall, R.E. was a nice man to work for. In some regards, he was perfect because he gave Grace all the freedom she needed to do what she thought was best. On the other hand, he was challenging because he wasn't focused very much on the part of the business she managed, didn't understand it any better than she did, and wasn't regimented in providing consistent communication, updates, feedback, or support. It was almost like he thought that if no one was complaining about them anymore, she must be doing okay. But Grace was never satisfied with just okay. Grace wanted to be great at all the things she worked on, so she was frequently frustrated that he didn't seem to care or make time for her. When Grace finally got to have her one-on-one meeting with him to discuss her first ninety-day progress report, he didn't really have too much to offer her in terms of feedback or next steps, with the exception that he felt that she had built a solid foundation and he thought the team meeting had gone well.

When she pushed on the issue of the two people she was considering firing, he was not encouraging. He didn't disagree that it needed to happen, but he discussed the politics involved, explaining that one person had influential friends in the company and had been there a long time and the other person everyone was afraid of. He shared that the previous manager had been unsuccessful in trying to fire her in the past and just gave up from lack of support. Grace asked if she would have his support if she moved forward with an exit strategy, and his response was a nebulous "yes."

Looking for more concrete direction, Grace then asked him specifically what he wanted her to do or focus on in the next ninety days. His exact words were, "I want you to do what you have done everywhere you have ever worked." Grace looked at him and said, "What does that mean?" His response was short and to the point. "I want you to make magic. This is a young and growing company with inexperienced leaders. I want you to show them what magic looks like."

Grace walked away again wondering what she had gotten herself into. "Make Magic." How in the world was she supposed to do that? She was confident in her abilities and she had a strong record of success, but up until now she had never been aware of any supernatural powers that she possessed that could magically influence the outcomes of her team.

Having successfully used the pig icon as a motivational tool for her team, Grace returned to her desk and began searching for something to motivate herself to find a way to conjure up some magic, and there it was—a picture of a big pig with this quote attached:

"I turn vegetables into bacon! What's your superpower?"

Grace went in search of her inner superpower, and she knew from her previous business experience exactly where she could find it. If R.E. wanted "magic," he would get it. She just needed to get him to agree to pay for it.

Grace decided, having recently come from the business, that what she needed was her own trainer who would help her find her inner superwoman. This would not only allow her to soar but would help her develop a team plan that would teach her pigs to fly!

GRACE HIRES HER OWN EXECUTIVE TRAINER

With the decision made to hire a trainer and the budget approved, the search began for the right person and qualities to achieve the magic needed. Grace was familiar with the fundamentals of executive training and had herself witnessed the impressive results she had helped businesses to achieve when she had personally trained them, so what she was looking for was someone to be her sounding board and mirror for reflection on doing the right things for her people. Grace wanted help in working with her strengths and weaknesses and ensuring the plan she had in place would indeed help her team achieve their goals. Just as she asked deeper-level questions of her people to find solutions, she wanted someone to ask those types of questions of her, monitor her progress, and ensure her own accountability to her team.

The night before Grace was going to meet with her new trainer for the first time, she couldn't sleep. How in the world was she going to explain to her trainer that what she needed her help with was learning to make magic? What does magic look like? Feel like? Result in? How can magic even be possible when magicians never reveal their secrets? How could the magic of Grace unfold in her own heart? She didn't know the answers to those questions, but she was about to find out in a big way!

Grace knew she was a winner in her heart by just having the courage to show up for the new job despite all her other challenges and then to a meeting and, with a straight face, to tell her new trainer, Dixie, that what she needed her help with was to "Make Magic." To her surprise, Dixie didn't laugh or judge when she said it. She just asked, "What type of magic are you looking to make?" That's when Grace unloaded all the details of her present situation: the players, the problems, what was at stake, and why she was so determined to be a success in her new role. Grace had never failed in anything she set her mind to doing, and she wasn't about to let this be the first time. It was an information dump of mega proportion with personal and professional issues discussed, and yet Dixie just sat there asking questions, making notes, and displaying empathy. As the session drew to a close, Dixie gave Grace homework to complete before the next meeting: define M-A-G-I-C by associating a word with each letter that would accomplish what she needed to accomplish in the next ninety days.

> **See Ground Rule #2:** Practice What You Preach. With this particular decision to seek outside counsel, Grace was demonstrating the vulnerability to admit that she didn't know how to make magic in this scenario, but she was confident enough to admit it, ask for help to define it, make a plan for it, and try her best to accomplish it. In other words, model the behavior in the way that encourages others to do the same.

This is how Grace decided to define M-A-G-I-C:

M e

A ttitude

G oals

I nitiative

C haracter

Magic starts and ends with me. It's my responsibility to set the standard that is deemed as exemplary behavior and performance. My attitude sets the tone for the team to follow. I must make critical connections with key influencers that can help my team improve their performance and achieve their goals. I must learn as much as I can about what they do so I can help them be better. I have to be honest, open, believable, trustworthy, and unafraid to take risks that will challenge the status quo. I must exemplify what success looks like by setting stretch goals for me and my team and being willing to work side by side with them to achieve them. I must initiate the change I want in them by first making the change in me. I need to be all in for this team before I ask them to be all in.

I must set the standard of quality and delivery. I must hire the best possible people to better my team. I must give the team the credit when we achieve success. I must always do the right thing, lead by example, promote servant leadership, and foster a can-do attitude with a fun- loving and caring spirit. I must be confident in myself and my ability to lead them.

Most managers do a lot of these things, but MAGIC happens when you do them all.

When they become more than just words and actions, those words and actions become who you are, what you believe, and how you approach life. MAGIC isn't easy. MAGIC isn't always comfortable. MAGIC requires that your actions come from your heart, and it means that you do the right thing not just sometimes but every time. MAGIC only happens when you commit and care.

"Self confidence is a superpower. Once you start to believe in yourself, magic starts happening."

— ANONYMOUS

READER PARTICIPATION & REFLECTION EXERCISES

"One of the oldest tricks that the universe plays on human beings is to bury STRANGE JEWELS deep within us all and then stand back and see if WE CAN EVER FIND THEM. The hunt to discover those jewels-that's creative living."

—ELIZABETH GILBERT

"And above all, watch with glittering eyes the whole world around you because the greatest secrets are always hidden in the most unlikely places. Those who don't believe in magic will never find it."

—ROALD DAHL

CHAPTER 4 LESSON: BELIEVE IN THE MAGIC WITHIN YOU

1. If given an assignment to "go make magic" at work, how would you define MAGIC?

2. Does Grace's definition of MAGIC—Me, Attitude, Goals, Initiative, and Character—fit this particular situation?

3. What would you say is Grace's superpower? What is yours?

4. How can your superpower be used to change a current work or personal situation you'd most like to change to achieve a positive outcome?

5. How do Grace's ice cream breaks and pig tchotchkes reinforce the team brand she is trying to build?

Chapter 5

EVERY DAY I'M TRUFFLIN'

"You gotta have a swine to show you where the truffles are"

—EDWARD ALBEE

Pigs and Truffles: are a rare and expensive fruiting body of a subterranean fungus. Italian white truffles go for up to nine thousand dollars per pound. They would be far more expensive even than that, were it not for the remarkable ability of trained pigs to sniff them out from as deep as three feet underground. It comes down to aroma, so much that it is often said that truffles are as much an aphrodisiac to humans as they are to the relentless pigs that pursue them. And that is nothing to snort about!

You are probably wondering: what in the world do pigs looking for truffles have to do with aeronautics? You'd be surprised. Sometimes MAGIC doesn't come to us. Sometimes we have to go out hunting for it.

Working with Dixie, Grace learned to do some painful soul searching—or in her case. "soul hunting." For example, Dixie had Grace answer these very important deeper-level questions: "When are you happy and at your best? And what does it mean to speak and live in truth and honesty?" I know trainers often speak in an esoteric or obscure language, but speaking from my own personal experience, if you truly search your soul for the answers, it's incredible what you can find out about yourself.

First, Grace sat down and made a list answering the questions about when she was at her best. Her answer was, "I am happy and at my best when I am using my business experience, skills, and creativity and sharing knowledge to help others have greater success in their work.

This brings me joy because I am helping them be their very best and achieve their personal and professional goals. I am the voice of reason and of possibility. I use my sense of humor, humility, servant leadership, and kindness to raise people up, lift their spirits, and help them believe anything is possible. I love to feel needed to help others be their best.

When I speak and live in truth and honesty, I make others feel special and I get to be the most genuine and authentic me."

After Grace looked at her answers, she had to admit to herself that she was doing a pretty good job of staying true to who she was. Having the open and intimate dialogue with the team about where everyone was coming from was exactly what the first step needed to be. Reading the story of "The Three Little Pigs" was a bit risky but fun, an authentic way to reveal her personality. She had spent a good deal of time analyzing the situation of where they were as a team. She had shared openly with the team her findings, and throughout the team meeting she had shared a strategic plan and empowered them to take ownership and action. Using the story as a metaphor for their work situation, knowing everyone's house was currently made of hay, she challenged them to put in the work and do it right from this point on to fortify their place in the company. Finally, giving them the piggy banks and trust fund dollars as a symbol of the team and her belief in them, displayed for all to see even before they earned it or believed it themselves, gave them accountability, hope, recognition, and motivation to want to do better. It also made them feel special and loved.

> **See Ground Rules of Leadership:** 1, 2, 3, & 4: Stay true to who you are, practice what you preach, love your team, stand up for them and show your strength, courage, and fortitude.

What needed to be addressed next was Grace's trust and belief that she herself had already gotten them to back out of the gate, and that they would be ready to start taxiing to the runway, ready to take flight when they were notified that they were next in line for takeoff!

F.L.Y. (FIRST LOVE YOURSELF)

"If you want to soar in life, you must first learn to love yourself; others will come next."

—MARK STERLING

The reason it is important to love yourself first is because that's where you find your self- confidence and self-worth, and in doing so you feel happy. Loving oneself is caring about oneself, taking responsibility for oneself, respecting oneself, and knowing oneself, meaning being realistic about one's strengths and weaknesses. Everyone has both.

Grace now knew that it was okay to put her desire to be needed and valued at the top of the list alongside the company's goal of her team needing to be better. She could treat her team as well as her own self with a little more gentleness, concern, and caring. She did not have to be perfect all the time, but it was okay to strive for it. Now the goals would be synergistic, not opposing.

Next Grace knew that she needed to identify the basic things she wanted to get out of the job. On the top of that list was feedback that what she was doing was making a difference. She would accept it and treasure it from the people she worked with and managed, as well as from the other departments her team served. Making a difference to them would be more valuable than making a difference in her career. Being seen as an inspiring leader by her peers or having other employees ask if they could come and work for her team would signify that she was making great progress.

Finally, Grace decided that since she had nothing to lose and everything to gain, she would go unfiltered. She would do more of the things that energized herself and her team, the very things that led Grace to be her very best self. She would improve upon her inner-voice conversation about what she didn't know, reinforce her positive contributions, and not try to fix and learn everything all at once.

OTHERS WILL COME NEXT!

Now that Grace felt comfortable that she was on track for success, she knew that two of her team members were not helping the team be their very best. The team morale was low in Hog Jaw because someone was always absent or leaving early due to not feeling well, which left the others to do more of his work, and in Hog D, there was an employee who would just bully everyone to get what she wanted. So Grace set up a strategy to get both of those employees looking for other careers. If Grace could pull that off and hire new people with the right attitude and skill set, the remaining team members would see and learn that if you do what you say you are going to do, you earn the respect and trust of others.

HOG JAW

Elvis Pigsley was indeed a smooth operator. Since he had been there from the very early stages of the company, he was well liked and connected, but he wasn't working his job, he was working the system. Elvis would often ask to leave early due to excruciating body pain that he said required frequent treatments to get relief, and sometimes it would take days for the relief to kick in, so in essence he would disappear for days. Grace was uncertain about the level of truth in this situation, so she decided to test it out in a harmless manner that would prove her suspicions either right or wrong.

Grace decided to invite her Hog Jaw team out for an evening out of burgers, beer, bowling, and bonding. A great time was had by all, filled with lots of competition, giggles, and bonding despite everyone's obvious differences. Most importantly, Grace's suspicion proved correct that Elvis was in fine physical and competitive form when it came to fun, just not when it came to working in the office on a regular basis.

With her suspicions in hand, Grace went to HR to get an opinion on the best way to proceed. They told her to have discussions with Elvis and document, document, document.

And then one day it happened: Grace got the lucky break she was waiting for when Elvis was out of the office on an out-of-town business trip, but he left early to come home due to an illness, without telling her. Then he posted a bizarre story on social media clearly indicating that he was home, he was well, but he was not working. Busted! Within a matter of a few days, with the help of HR, Elvis had left the building for good.

HOG D

Now Grace could turn her attention to the situation in Hog D, knowing full well how difficult and tricky that situation might become. Barbie was smart, tenured in her position, and not afraid to be a bit of a bully. People were afraid of her. Grace needed to stay strong because this was the best decision for her team to get better.

So Grace asked Dixie for some guidance on how to be strong and empathetic at the same time. As it turned out, after Grace did her homework on strength vs. empathy, it was exactly what this situation called for.

If empathy is the ability to put oneself into the shoes of another and understand their feelings and perspectives, then Grace knew that she needed to understand what drove Barbie to behave the way she did.

> *"Empathy is a choice and it's a vulnerable choice.*
> *In order to connect with you, I have to connect with*
> *something in myself that knows that feeling."*
>
> **—BRENÉ BROWN**

Everyday Grace was "trufflin'" to find the answers that would help make her team work at peak performance. That meant every player needed to be committed, not just involved in doing their job or just showing up to the office.

Grace began the process of moving Barbie to the realization that she didn't really want to work there anymore by sitting down and talking with her about her career there. She asked questions like when she had started there, what she did, what she liked about the company, what had changed over time, what the things that frustrated her were, and most importantly, how she believed others perceived her.

Barbie was taken by surprise by this approach and didn't really know how to respond except to be open and vulnerable as well with her answers. She knew her job was in jeopardy, so she was more ready to be berated than she was to be spoken to as a human being with real feelings, emotions, stories, and concerns.

Barbie had loved working there back in the good ol' days when it was just a small group of people and everyone played a key role in the company's survival. She felt valued and important then, and the customers she had were some of the originals that did business with the company. But then everything changed. The business grew, and they kept adding more people, and each individual felt valued less and less. She resented, as a more mature, experienced woman, having to train younger inexperienced people. So many of the original people had "poofed" or disappeared. She was a single, middle-aged woman supporting herself and feared more than anything that she was becoming irrelevant to new technology and to millennials. She was angry and hurt that it wasn't like it used to be, but she wasn't willing to share what she knew.

Grace shared some of her work experiences, including broken promises, technology challenges, and fears, with Barbie, and soon they both realized they had more in common than they had thought. The bottom line soon became clear, though: the job required that she share her accounts and her knowledge, and she needed to channel her anger or move on, as Grace had herself done earlier in her career. At the end of the day, there was a job that needed to be done, and she needed to embrace who was in charge and how things were to be handled. At the end of ninety days, Barbie chose not to embrace change or accept that being angry or not liking the way things were being done was not a substitute for knowledge she did not want to share. Some would say she was fired. Grace believed that, with all the requirements clearly spelled out and with a willing supporter to help her adjust, Barbie self-selected to depart by refusing to accept that the team was moving forward, not living in the past.

> **See Ground rule #2:** Practice what you preach. For Grace, failure in this part of the plan was not an option. The two employees discussed were holding the rest of the team back by continuing to not buy into the new team plan, doing no work thereby adding to the burden of the rest of the teammates. Grace gave every opportunity for Barbie and Elvis to accept the changes, and ask for help, but for whatever reasons they just couldn't or wouldn't. Grace had to make the tough call to let them both go to demonstrate to the rest of the team that everyone had to be all in.

READER PARTICIPATION & REFLECTION EXERCISES

"Don't look for things.to be easier, look for you to be better"

—JIM ROHN

LESSONS LEARNED IN CHAPTER 5:

- Magic and truffles don't come easily or cheaply.

- Sometimes you have to hunt or search within yourself to find the answers you seek.

1. Think of a time and place when you were at your best. What did that look like, and how were you doing it?

2. What were the skills and gifts you were using then, and how does that make you feel?

3. **FLY:** First Love Yourself! It's okay to have needs and want them to be met; however, you may have to shift your mind about who can meet those needs satisfactorily for you at that moment in time. Do you know what you need to be at your best? Who in your life currently meets those needs?

4. How do you know when it's time to cut the cord with those who aren't on the same page as you personally or professionally?

SWINE FLEW

> *"When you come to the edge of the light you know and are about to step off into the darkness of the unknown, faith is knowing two things will happen: There will be something to stand on, or you will be taught to fly."*
>
> **—PATRICK OVERTON**

> *"I wonder if anyone actually sat down and thought about how much stuff is going to happen when pigs learn to fly?"*
>
> **—UNKNOWN**

The house Grace was building was now getting stronger, replacing the straw that was weak with more solid sticks, when she added Piggy Azalea in Hog Jaw and Taylor Swine in Hog Dawg.

Finally, she had a team of people that all wanted to be with the team and could buy into what she was building.

Everyone was working hard at getting better in their roles, improving the quality of their work, and strengthening the trust and reliability they had with each other as well as with the internal and external customers they serviced. When someone came down with a case of swine flu that caused them to be away from work for a variety of personal reasons (multiple pregnancies, deaths in the family, personal tragedies, or illness), and Grace had multiple cases of swine flu in both offices in her tenure, the other team members picked up the sticks for the team members that were hurt and kept the house together, no matter how hard people tried to blow it down. And they did!

Her business grew so much that she was even able to make another addition to the sales team in Chris P. Bacon in Hawg Jaw, and later her department became a training ground for all customer service team members that wanted to learn how to sell, not just service aeronautics customers, when she added Pork Chop in Hog Jaw and Pig Achu in Hog Dawg. A house of bricks was on the horizon. Grace could feel it all coming together.

But the team didn't just work hard, they played hard too, with adventures that helped coworkers become family.

Besides the piggy banks and trust fund dollars, one of the next things Grace did with the team was The Pig Personality Profile (By Gordon Cotton, Trainer, Marine Atlantic, Inc.). It was in no way a scientific assessment but rather an icebreaker for a team meeting—good for laughs and to get her team members thinking about how their peers saw themselves and how the depictions they drew gave insight into their personalities. It was also good practice for the next team building activity in Hawg Dog, which was painting the three pigs on an actual canvas to be hung in their cubicles to keep the positive momentum going. They laughed, painted, bonded, and started to believe in themselves like they never had before.

Grace could see the culture within her team changing right before her eyes. She knew that the culture of any organization was its heart. With every beat, life was spreading throughout the body, feeding each cell with energy and the nourishment to support and sustain the organization. Without a heart, it's just a business. "If you believe in your heart that you are meant to live a life full of passion, purpose, magic, and miracles, you surely will," Grace told her team.

In all the years Grace Fully had worked, and in all the different types of businesses, she had witnessed many types of company cultures. Cultures of winning, cultures of complacency, cultures of survival of the fittest or of being the best at any price, but the ones Grace experienced that tended to be the most successful were focused on their people being treated as their greatest asset and doing the right things for them and the customers always.

> *"Culture is observational, not aspirational. It's not what you say, it's what you do."*
>
> **—MARC RANDOLPH**

The culture she was creating in her own team was built on trust. Grace knew she didn't need to be the expert on everything. Instead, she had to know who the expert was, build relationships with them, give more than she took, and always acknowledge the help when it was given.

The culture we create has to have rules with rewards and consequences, and the leader has to always do the right thing, even when it hurts or is unpopular.

> *"How will you know if something is the right thing to do? It's easier than you think, because if you listen to your heart, it will never lie to you."*
>
> **—ABBY VEGA**

GRACE FULLY

Grace Fully was not what you'd expect in a typical manager. That was the most remarkable aspect of her leadership. She was unexpected. She couldn't be described; she needed to be experienced. She looked at things differently, spoke differently, and carried herself in a way that made people curious as to what she was all about. Her words were different from what you'd expect to hear in a boardroom: she wouldn't say what you wanted to hear; she would say what you needed to know. When she spoke, people typically wanted to hear what she had to say because she who appeared weakest had become the cornerstone of her team. Grace was full of surprises. It was not just what was in her but what she was able to call forth in everyone around her: that you were way more than you thought you could be or told you were capable of.

Whenever things got particularly stressful you might find her in her cube writing poetry that put into words what she was thinking, or what would be needed to fix a certain situation. For some it looked like she was playing but the team quickly learned that it was just her way of problem solving, and a way to compartmentalize all the issues she was dealing with personally and professionally.

When she talked, it was not about technology or aeronautics, it was about the individual, the family, and the obstacles that were keeping your heart from singing.

Grace Fully was a pig, for goodness sake. She was not some thin, tall, supermodel in designer clothes or a superhero in disguise. She didn't care about what people saw on the outside. She cared about who you are on the inside. Grace was showing up now in her role to see who she truly was, helping to put everyone she encountered in the flow of life. She helped people see that work and home are not separate parts but part of a total package. Grace reminded people that the whole package includes your head, heart, hands, skills, knowledge, expertise, and a balance of work and family. Grace, despite all of her burdens personal and professional, believed that God would ultimately give her the strength for whatever she needed to face, enable her to have the power to fix what needed to be fixed, and the ability to accomplish what she could not by her own means. It would simply be divine.

Grace created magic! She created the culture wherever she went. Grace was more interested in caring about people, not in caring about what people's opinion of her were. Grace was full, fully herself. Not full of herself—true to herself, and what she brought to people would help them find their truth.

Grace's truth was known and accepted by her team. They knew the value Grace brought to the table, but they also knew that Grace was not technically up to speed on every aspect of the three distinct businesses they managed, and it bothered Grace deeply despite her not even being in the job six months yet. So Grace decided to call upon her trusted Team Lead in Hawg D, Gwin, to make sure what she was seeing and believing was also real to the team members as well. When Grace asked if Gwin thought all her teammates were buying in and believing that the path Grace had laid out for them was bringing them together, holding them accountable, giving them what they needed and desired, and making a difference to the customers they served, Gwin was excited to be valued enough to share her thoughts on the subject. "The thing I like best about you, Grace, is that you came in with a totally different perspective on how a business/team should run," she said. "You acknowledged from the beginning that despite your manager title, we all needed to be thought of and treated as equals because we all had knowledge and expertise in subject matters that no one else had, and to make the whole department work we needed to trust each other as specialists in our respective fields. You also showed care and concern about us as individuals, wanted to know what was important to us, showed interest in our families, career aspirations, and fears, and trusted us to be adept enough to teach each other about our businesses, experiences in life, and how to be better in-dividuals and team players. Because you couldn't answer all the technical questions in Senior-level meetings, you brought us along and gave us exposure we never would have had without you. Finally, because you recognized that we were siloed and separated by distance, you worked hard at bringing us together face-to-face for work and fun, and so far you've delivered on every promise you've made. You were honest and transparent from the beginning, Grace, and now we believe in ourselves and we believe in you and where you are trying to take us. You really are not like any manager we've ever had. Does that help?" It took Grace a few minutes to process what she had just heard from Gwin, and then she hugged her and thanked her for her honest and genuine feedback. The "flight plan" to success was indeed working!

Once you have found yourself speaking your truth, and others telling it back to you accept all that you are, believe you are capable of anything and are ready to take action. You can fly.

"I teach pigs to fly!"

—GRACE FULLY

CREATING A CULTURE OF SUCCESS

Just one more note on the importance of culture in an organization. According to Peter Drucker, noted American management consultant, educator, and author, *"Culture eats strategy for breakfast, lunch and dinner every time."*

The senior leaders you hire for your organization are the keepers or caretakers of the company culture. They champion its identity and protect the culture to keep the company's competitive edge.

But what if the company culture is bad? Grace believes that if you do these six things, you will still win:

1. Ask questions, and then listen openly for honest, open, genuine feedback, not people telling you what they think you want to hear.

2. Never seek the glory of the success your team has. Empower your team by giving them the glory of success.

3. Have the courage to ask your direct reports for feedback on yourself. Does my behavior increase or decrease your trust in me?

4. Channel the self-ego of all the team's individuals in a positive way.

5. Be vulnerable without fear. It makes you human.

6. Trust your team even before they earn it because you accept and believe in their abilities to be the experts in their jobs. You're not the expert on everything!

IT'S THE CULTURE YOU CREATE

The culture of an organization begins in the heart
Everyone knows that at least everyone that's smart
With every beat its energy and life that's spread
And how those that can make magic chose to be led

Like its people, each business culture is diverse
And understanding that difference happens when you converse
The leader must exemplify the code of its conduct
And remove everything that impedes the ability to construct

Once the team is chosen and understands their roles
And has all the necessary tools to make their goals
It's really quite incredible what a great culture brings
Going from just good to great ensures everyone earns their wings

— GRACE FULLY

READER PARTICIPATION & REFLECTION EXERCISES

"One of our values is that you should be looking out for each other. Everyone should try to make the lives of everyone else who works here a little bit simpler."

—STEWART BUTTERFIELD

CHAPTER 6 LESSON: THE CULTURE YOU CREATE BEGINS IN YOUR HEART

1. What were the signs her team and company gave Grace that reinforced that the house they were building was getting stronger?

2. How did the Pig Personality Profile and painting "The Three Little Pigs" and hanging the paintings in the cubicle strengthen the team and the culture? What do you do to positively impact the culture where you live or work?

3. Describe in your own words what you'd look and feel like if you were fully living in "Grace"?

4. What are the six steps of Creating a Culture of Success?" How comfortable on a scale of 1-5 are you to follow Grace's steps where you live and work? Why?

CASTING PEARLS
BEFORE SWINE

"Do not give dogs what is sacred. Do not throw your pearls to pigs. If you do, they may trample them under their feet and tear you to pieces."

—MATTHEW 7:6

"People may hear your words but they will feel your attitude."

—JOHN C. MAXWELL

In its simplest form, the Matthew Bible verse basically translates into this: do not persist in offering what is sacred or of value to those who have no appreciation for it because not only will your gift become contaminated and disrespected, your generous efforts could be rebuffed or perhaps even openly attacked.

Everything was going better than Grace could have ever imagined. Her employees were getting recognized, a few promotions were given to her team members and looking back, even Grace couldn't believe how far everyone had come in just seven short months. It was now time for Grace and R.E. to meet up for her long-awaited six-month review.

See Ground Rule of Leadership: #5, Always put their success before your own. It was one Grace's deepest held tenets, that her own success would be obvious and rewarded if she put her team's success before her own, gave them the recognition, got them promoted, and demonstrated the behaviors she wanted others to follow. It was time to find out if it was true here.

Grace looked forward to this meeting, feeling as if she had far exceeded anyone's expectations of what was possible with a group that everyone had wanted her to fire and start all over again. Perhaps she too might be recognized now for her accomplishments, she thought as R.E. had promised her in the interview and again in their first meeting the week she started.

The review began on a positive note with R.E. saying how pleased he was with everything she was doing, how well the team was working together, and the buzz on the floor of how much fun the team was having while getting things done in a timely and accurate fashion. He acknowledged Grace's accomplishment of purging her team of negative employees and filling the slots with promising new talent. In summary, he had nothing to critique her on. Upper management was taking notice and felt that her team was finally on the right track, and while Grace's leadership skills and style were unprecedented in the aeronautics industry, it seemed to work well for them. Momentum was building, and maybe even a tad bit of competitive jealousy from other teams existed because of the fun Grace's team was having while those other teams had managers that clearly and comfortably stayed in the box. R.E. agreed the team was making Magic and that Grace should keep doing what she was doing.

"Wow," said Grace. "That is amazing feedback, and I am tickled pink that we are finally getting some good attention and recognition. So I guess the million dollar question, then, is "Have I proven myself enough as an effective leader in these seven months to attain the Director title and salary increase you promised when I first started?"

R.E. sighed and hesitated a moment before he spoke, initially refusing to make eye contact. When he finally spoke, he said, "No, the senior leadership team would like to see you execute a big project outside of managing your team. In fact, it's a company-wide initiative around fundraising, and they want you to be the chairperson for both locations." Grace looked at him and said, "Is this something I can refuse since I'm still learning my day job? This sounds like another full-time job on top of the one I already have. You do realize that my mother is dying of cancer in my home as we speak. And I have absolutely no experience in fundraising, nor is it part of my job description." R.E. responded, "Unfortunately not, some companies ask for volunteers, but we are a "voluntold" company. You can't refuse, but if you do this well, by the end of the year I'm sure great things will be on the horizon for you."

"The reward for good work is more work"

—TOM SACHS

Grace left the meeting feeling disappointed and betrayed. It wasn't that Grace wasn't appreciative of all opportunities for growth and development and trying new things, it was just that between work and her home life Grace felt like she was being penalized with more work for having done a great job thus far. Every time Grace thought she was making a difference, doing a good job, and creating a culture of integrity and accountability, she felt blindsided that her senior leadership team didn't know or care about her as a person. Being "voluntold" about what hoop she had to jump through next seemed more like a punishment than any type of recognition.

"How in the world am I going to rally myself to do this after feeling so disappointed, taken advantage of, and let down," she thought. "My stomach feels like the first day I walked in the door. Oh, good grief, what to do? What to do?"

DIXIE DUST

Grace knew her attitude would definitely need an adjustment. She knew everyone dealt with disappointments—it's just part of life.

> *"Five of the best ways to deal with disappointment*
> *are: let it out, get a different perspective on it, know*
> *your own heart, practice positive self-talk, and don't*
> *let it fester, think about it and move on."*
>
> **—MAGGIE WOOLL**

Still, she thought, "Why even bother to try anymore? No one cares. No one keeps their word. But most importantly, no one values the cultural shift of accountability, teamwork, recognition, joy, and pride in a job well done that I brought to the team. In fact, it seems to be working against them. Like, how dare they be happy and successful at work? 'Voluntold' is just an ugly, cowardly way for a company to say "screw you."

When Grace next met with her trainer, Dixie, she was beside herself. She just needed to get her frustration off her chest and get another perspective on the situation because all Grace was feeling was how arbitrary it seemed that the assignment of the new project came at the exact time the promise R.E. had made was broken, how cruel this new project was at this point in her job and family situation at home, and how challenging it was to work in an environment where the culture was to just say "No, not yet, but we'd like for you to do this to be considered next time."

Dixie listened as she always did and then asked Grace one question: "So what do you want to do about it?" At first Grace responded "Quit!" Then Dixie reminded Grace that all of her greatest achievements in life had happened when others would have quit but she kept going. "Yes, I'm aware, but I'm also aware that sometimes no matter how hard you try, you can't get someone to value what is not in them."

Then Dixie said, "Just for one minute, I want you to imagine if you did do it: what would it look like, and how would you want others to feel while you were doing it?" Oh, how Grace hated those questions!

Those were the trick questions that got you so angry or inspired that you threw everything at her to show that you could do something and blow the doors off it, but you just didn't want to at that moment. So Grace sat with her arms folded and her mouth shut in silence. Dixie sat in silence too. That was even more frustrating than the previous question. The ability to sit still in silence until a proper response is given is an old sales tactic. Whoever speaks first loses, and Dixie wasn't about to let Grace off the hook.

So Grace gave in and spoke first. She said, "The problem with doing this fundraising thing is that it's just one more thing that employees are "voluntold" to do. There is no creativity, no guidelines on what to do or how to do it, and no budget for it. Everyone is just told what day to enroll and to give more than they did last year. Who is inspired by that kind of directive?" So Dixie then asked, "What would you want to do differently to change that mindset and attitude?"

Grace replied, "I'd want them to help the donors understand why we support this charity, who they were impacting, and how it helped them. Maybe they could meet someone who was benefitting from the programs they offered. I'd want to be able to reach into every individual's body and touch their heart specifically to fully realize how blessed they were and how important it was for them to give back to those less fortunate. I'd want every individual to feel the joy of what phenomenal success felt like because everyone did their part in making it happen."

Now it was Dixie who sat silently, digesting the power in what Grace had just said. "Wow, you have given this some deep thought, and your strategy is remarkable, so why won't you do it?" Grace answered, "Because they won't appreciate or value the effort it would take to do it—they'd be just as happy with a two percent increase over last year." "So then," Dixie said, "Don't do it for them. Do it for you, your team, and the people whose lives would be positively impacted by the money you raised. Show them the Magic of Grace Fully in all her glory and the power that has over everyone whose life you touch in the process."

Grace stood to leave after the training session was over, still with a heavy heart and a bit wary of the reaction to the plan she was formulating in her brain, but she knew without a doubt that what she was about to do would change the way the company did this event forever. She'd be leaving her mark forever on this organization, and that was acknowledgement enough for Grace.

She thanked Dixie again for her counsel and wisdom and warned her that after she was done, she'd either be fired or promoted for sure.

READER PARTICIPATION & REFLECTION EXERCISES

*"Life is a matter of making choices, and
every choice you make makes you!"*

—JOHN C. MAXWELL

CHAPTER 7 LESSON: LIFE PRESENTS US WITH MANY CHOICES. THE CHOICES WE MAKE DETERMINE OUR FUTURE

1. In this chapter, Grace was given her greatest challenge yet. She could have said no and refused to do it claiming personal reasons. Why do you think she didn't back down? Have you ever been given a tough choice when you did back down? Would you change it knowing what you know now?

2. What message was the company trying to signal to Grace? Why?

3. What role did Dixie the Executive Trainer play in solidifying what Grace already knew in her heart she would do?

4. Without reading ahead, can you predict how the outcome of this decision will manifest itself?

Part Three

PRACTICE
AND ENJOY

TO THE HEAVENS ON THE
WINGS OF A PIG

—JOHN STEINBECK

"If you are going to get the pigs you'll need back-up. They are nothing to be truffled with!"

—K.M. RANDALL

"Do not follow where the path may lead. Go instead where there is no path and leave a trail."

- RALPH WALDO EMERSON

John Steinbeck was told by one of his professors that he would become an author when pigs fly, which is why he imprinted on all of his thirty-three published books the symbol of a winged pig surrounded by the Latin phrase "ad astra peralia porci" meaning "to the heavens on the wings of a pig."

Grace came back to work the next day on fire! The first thing she did was ask Babe to order wolf noses with elastic bands to put on all the piggy banks to remind everyone of the wolves that were lurking amongst them. Everyone knew what the three little pigs represented. But will taking your time to do something right eventually pay off, and what about the wolf? The wolf represents greed and vengeance, the desire for revenge. Now that it was apparent that the twigs were being replaced with bricks, the wolf would surely come knocking. It was not the first costume accessory the piggy banks would wear, nor would it be the last. They got dressed for Halloween and Christmas and whenever the mood struck Grace or a team member to tighten up the team spirit. It was all done in fun, but it served a purpose, and that purpose was to signify that they were a united team always. No one could blow that house down!

Then Grace set up a meeting with the CEO to clarify what the goals, objectives, deliverables, timeframes, guidelines, and budgets were to run this campaign. The CEO said that she had never been asked that before — people just did it. Grace also shared what she felt the core fund raising activities should be and why. Grace asked if there were a few former campaign managers she could talk to glean from them best practices, and again she was told by the CEO, Petunia Squiggles, "They just do the best they can!" Petunia mentioned, however, before Grace left the office, that the success of the campaign was critical to the company and its image within the community. Otherwise, it was Godspeed and good luck!

Next Grace met with a couple of the previous campaign managers to pick their brains, and they were very kind in sharing their thoughts on the campaign and the selection of the campaign manager. It boiled down to: if no one volunteers, someone is "voluntold." Just try to do better than last year. No, there are no notes, but we have done blah, blah, blah…And if we can help in any way, we will, we've all been stuck doing this for years.

At eight months in, Grace was not at all surprised anymore by what little information, support, or advice she was given. Grace decided then and there that she was going to blow it out of the water, no matter what it took, and that she would use this challenge as the ultimate team- building experience. No matter how things ended, this project, this campaign, this test of character would be Grace's legacy!

Apathy (noun) is a lack of feeling, emotion, interest, and concern. Apathy is a state of indifference, or the suppression of emotions such as concern, excitement, motivation, or passion.

Whatever the definition, it was endemic in this company culture like Grace had never experienced or witnessed before. Even if it was the last thing she did there, Grace was determined to make everyone in the organization, even if just for one moment, care, feel pride, experience joy, and have the happiness of knowing that through their participation in this campaign they made a difference because someone touched their heart.

CAMPAIGN STRATEGY

Grace went back to her desk that afternoon and put together an outline of what it would take to knock this fundraiser out of the park. She pulled out a sheet of paper, made five boxes, and entitled them:

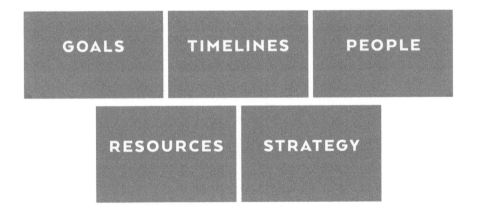

GOALS

1. Touch the heart of every employee in both offices in some way that encourages participation.

2. Beat last year's financial contribution goal to charity.

3. Increase participation rate to 100%

TIMELINE

1. September–November

2. Create a three-month calendar of events from kick-off to registration and contribution day

PEOPLE

1. Grace as a leader will own it!

2. Create an atmosphere of fun so that people will want to volunteer.

3. Utilize and coordinate her team in both offices to support the campaign and turn it into the ultimate team-building opportunity.

4. Gain support of Sr. Leadership to participate and set a good example.

RESOURCES

1. Seek guidance on budget restrictions.

2. Creatively think of what no one else ever thought of before.

STRATEGY

1. Bring it to the people.

2. Help them understand why.

3. Frequent communication

4. Indelibly touch their hearts.

5. Make it fun.

Grace then gathered her team and explained the scope of the assignment that she had just been given. Grace was a straight shooter, so she was honest about how she felt, the challenges she was facing, the expectations that were being put upon her, and her hope that they would volunteer to help. She would not make her team help, but she hoped they would unite and offer themselves as a solution.

To her extreme delight, they expressed that they knew what was going on and were not surprised by what she had shared. They were all disappointed but not surprised that Grace did not receive the promised promotion. And for the very first time, they agreed to pull together and have her back on this. If it was a challenge for one team member, it was a challenge they'd all face together. Bring it on! Grace was in tears over how much they had developed and how strong they had become as a team. She had never felt greater pride than in that moment. Not only was everything going to be okay, everything was never going to be the same again!

READER PARTICIPATION & REFLECTION EXERCISES

"Throw me to the wolves, and I'll return leading the pack."

—UNKNOWN

CHAPTER 8 LESSON: "BRICKS ARE INDEPENDENT BUT CAN WORK WELL WITH OTHERS, TOUGH TO CRACK, FIERCELY LOYAL, AND PUT IN THE RIGHT SPOT WILL HOLD ANYTHING THAT YOU'VE EVER HELD DEAR WITH THE GREATEST OF EASE."

—NICOLE MCKAY

1. How did the accessories for the piggy banks reinforce the unity of the team and strengthen the will of the team?

2. What role did the wolf nose play in gaining an all-in commitment from the team?

3. How do you deal with people at work or in your own personal life who are apathetic to things that are important to you?

4. How did the structure of the five-step plan—Goals, Timelines, People, Resources, and Strategy—cement the ultimate success of this endeavor?

Chapter 9

IN A PIG'S EYE

*U.S. slang used to express scornful disbelief
that something cannot happen.*

—MERRIAM-WEBSTER

Never, under no circumstances, and emphatic disbelief were all the expressions people made about Grace and her team's chances of being successful at their latest assignment. For most employees of the company, the fundraiser was just another one of those things you had to endure. The same people were tapped to execute aspects of the task yearly, but like Grace they had full-time jobs to do as well. This year, Grace heard that someone else had been slated to do the task but had insisted that she couldn't possibly do it because of personal circumstances, and then that's when Grace became the designate. It didn't seem to matter that Grace had a terminally ill parent at home as a personal circumstance. But Grace was more than determined than ever that this would be the team's finest hour and that their impact would be felt throughout the entire organization for many years to come. Grace dutifully briefed the CEO as to what she had planned out and was given the okay to move forward.

With her campaign strategy in hand, Grace and her teams in Hog Jaw and Hog Dawg began to put details, activities, and timeframes in place. Grace worked with her team leads in both offices to coordinate simultaneous events. If this was going to be the success they imagined and planned for, it would have to start off at the simultaneous monthly all-employee meeting in September and clearly make the statement that this was not going to be "your momma's fundraising campaign." It was going to be new, exciting, and edgy, and it would touch every employee in a way they had never imagined.

THE CUPCAKE CHARADE

On the day of the September all-employee call, it was pre-planned that Senior leadership would wave the official flag that the campaign was starting, set the expectations, and encourage participation and giving. They were also asked to announce that free cupcakes would be available to all in the break rooms in both locations after the call was finished so that employees were encouraged to come down to meet the campaign advisors and hear in detail what was going to take place during the next three months.

Toward the end of the call, an all-employee email was sent out saying that someone had stolen the cupcakes from the break rooms. You could hear the collective murmuring around the building wondering who would do such a thing and why. Everyone was reassured that the campaign team was on it and an update would be provided as soon as it was available.

By the time the call was ending, sure enough, the cupcakes were recovered, and everyone was asked to go and partake at once. What they didn't know was that when they came to the break rooms, they would find a prison cell stage set complete with bars and with male and female-sized prison stripe costumes for people to wear to get their very own mugshot taken. "The Cupcake Charade" had of course been set up by Grace and her team the whole time, and the Kick-Off mugshots could be placed on a company logoed coffee mug for purchase, with half of the proceeds going to cover the mug and the other half to the charity for the fundraiser. Most everyone wanted one, and absolutely no one could stop talking about the campaign and what had just happened. It was a great kick-off moment, and Grace and her team were just getting started!

> *"Go to the people. Live with them. Learn from them. Love them. Start with what they know. Build with what they have. But with the best leaders, when the work is done, the task accomplished, the people will say 'We have done this ourselves.'"*
>
> **—LAO TZU**

NOMADIC NOSHES

> *"Food brings people together on many different levels. It's nourishment of the soul and body; it's truly love."*
>
> **– GIADA DE LAURENTIIS**

Next up were the nomadic noshes in both locations! The employees were busy, and they spent most of their days with their faces buried in a computer monitor. There was no food available in the buildings where Grace and her team worked. To eat meant either bringing it from home or going out to get it, and that took time and money. So the team decided to purchase stainless steel service carts and stock them with snacks like gum, mints, nuts, and homemade baked goods and a cooler with water, soda, energy drinks, etc. Each day at about 11 a.m., one or two of the team members steered the cart through each department, offering goodies for sale at very reasonable prices in both locations. All profits made were donated to the fundraising campaign.

It was an instant and ingenious success with the employees! Besides bringing the basics to their offices, it broke down barriers and gave the team the opportunity to meet every employee, know their names, and know if they were sweet or salty types and water or energy drinkers, and that knowledge ultimately gave Grace and the team a personal peek into their unique personality and a better understanding on how to approach them when they needed their help to solve a problem. People gave special requests to add flavor preferences and even asked when their teams could take a week to push the cart so that they too could know everyone that worked there and help the team be more successful in the fundraising endeavor.

Without a doubt, the favorite items were homemade breads, cookies, cakes, and the like. Nothing says love like a slice of homemade banana bread. Grace and her team found that their coworkers were more than willing to bring in their own specialty items and wait for the reviews to come in, like when the employees asked for more and wanted to know who created that delicious treat.

It's safe to say that by this point Grace's team was getting their message out daily and touching people's hearts.

WALKING WITH PURPOSE

Taylor Swine on the Hog Dawg team came up with a wonderful idea about how to serve snacks but also keep the team's friends and peers healthy at the same time. She said, "What if we communicated the idea that we wanted to start walking our way to good health since the corporate health screening fair didn't actually give everyone the results they were looking for?" The idea was simple: register to participate, pay a small fee, get a company logo pedometer to record your steps daily, find a walking buddy, and go get your 10,000 steps per day. The goal was set at one million steps for both locations. Things took off quickly, and people were walking, talking, having fun, staying healthy, and competing against each other as the team recorded the weekly totals and published the results. By the end of the campaign, employees had logged over 16 million Purposeful Strides collectively, and those that participated had the t-shirt to prove it.

BELIEVE IN THE CAUSE/MEET THE BENEFICIARIES

Giving makes us happy. But are all donors the same? No, they are not. To transform a fundraising campaign, you need to understand all the reasons why a person chooses to donate. Once you understand the psychology of donating to charity, you can revolutionize your results.

> *"The Millennial Impact Project studied why donors across different generations give. Unexpectedly, according to the researcher, Derrick Feldmann, donors first give because they want to belong. They desire to join their friends or be part of a cause doing the good they wish to see in the world. As they gain that sense of belonging and begin to believe in the cause, they can be motivated to give more when the nonprofit taps into their giving style."*

—NETWORKFORGOOD

Grace and the team reached out to their local charity ambassadors and expressed to them that they had an idea to do something different to impact the campaign's outcome—something that had never been done before. They all felt that if their company teammates could actually hear from people who had benefited from the funds raised in years past, they would know then in their hearts that they were helping to change people's lives, not just doing something they felt pressured to do.

And so for the October All-Team Meeting, when business was finished being discussed, a beneficiary of funds from the charities in Hawg Dawg and one from Hawg Jaw got on the phone and shared their stories. Out of respect for privacy, no names or family details were given, but their personal stories of tragedy and human suffering touched every person listening in, especially when they thanked everyone for all they were doing to provide aid for them and their families. With tears dripping down everyone's faces as they drifted back to their offices, they now could put a person, a story, a tragedy, a why, to every dollar they might consider donating.

To keep the team spirit going, Grace and the team then instituted Monday and Friday team Jersey Days if people were willing to pay a small fee of $5 to be a bit more casual in their dress for work. The impact of this was that the team spirit was now evident throughout each department, in both locations and it was obvious that it was catching on.

WIN GREAT STUFF/ON-LINE AUCTION

Coming down the home stretch of the campaign, Grace's team implemented an online auction that was a continuation of a tactic used in previous campaigns. Employees in both locations were asked to go to local businesses and obtain gift certificates for free food, services, BOGO'S, special discounts, or just free stuff! Team members were looking specifically for football tickets, college or professional, free or reduced price rounds of golf, days off with pay, rounds of golf with an Exec, sports memorabilia, other collectibles, company logoed apparel, lunch with a Sr. Executive, baked goods, etc. The only limitation was imagination—that and the fear of asking for free things.

The auction ran online all day so people could scope out the merchandise in between meetings and work and put their bids in anytime they wanted. Of course, the last five minutes of the auction was when ninety-nine percent of the activity happened, as bids were made, then outbid, and then made again. In the end, there were both cries of joy and exasperation as the time ran out and winners of the items were notified.

After the money was collected for the items and prizes were awarded, photos were taken of the lucky prize holders and posted in the company newsletter.

TAKING THE PLUNGE

"Ninety nine percent of leadership failures are failures of character."

-GEN. HERBERT NORMAN SCHWARZKOPF, JR.

The "piece de resistance" is the most noteworthy or prized feature, aspect, event, or article of a series or group or attractions.

In this case, "Taking the Plunge" was the "pig de resistance" of the fundraising campaign. It was being held in Hog Jaw since this was where all the highest-ranking executives kept their offices. Grace and the team had already done an amazing job of raising funds through all the other activities, but this one was critical because it was the last one being held before the team would be asking for actual pledge donations for the next year and attempting to achieve a one hundred percent participation goal.

The idea behind it was to offer a catered outdoor picnic-style lunch for a fee along with providing a carnival-like atmosphere featuring a "Take the Plunge" challenge, in which each department head could be voted for with money by their direct reports to take a turn in a plunge tank. It was all about fun, team bonding, humility, responsibility, confidence, passion, and character. These are all qualities the greatest leaders possess. It's called taking one for the team, meaning willingly undertaking an unpleasant task or making a personal sacrifice for the collective benefit of one's friends or colleagues. Grace and the team thought that it was an excellent way not only to have fun but also to show another side to the company's leaders, letting their teams see them humble themselves for just a brief moment for the good of the team with the charity gaining the greatest benefit. After all, Grace had been told by the CEO when being assigned to the fundraiser "that the success of the campaign was critical for the image of the company in the community."

As the day of the event drew near, it was decided that all the team leads or managers that willingly volunteered or were voted by their teams would go first. The last person in would be the one Senior Executive voted on by their peers to represent the spirit of the whole campaign of "being all in."

Never in our wildest imaginations could we envision what was to happen next.

The voting on the Senior Executives included a list of all of the members of the leadership team and happened the day before the event. Every vote was one dollar and was done anonymously by computer, but everyone in the company could see how the trends were tracking as the results were updated every ten minutes. However, Grace had already spoken with HR and agreed that no woman would go in the tank so as not to create a "wet t-shirt" atmosphere, thus taking away from the fundamental good the activity was intended to create.

Early indicators had the VP of HR, the oldest member of the team and one who was retiring at the end of year, being the favorite, followed closely by the president of the company and the female VP who had approached Grace in the elevator earlier in the year. As she sat there with Babe and a few close cube mates, Grace's phone started ringing with votes as well as pleas to please not let them be chosen because they were spending three hundred dollars that evening to get their hair done or for some other reason they just couldn't do it. Subtle hints of ramifications for Grace and her team were even implied if certain outcomes were not changed. Tensions were high on the floor as results were being tallied and posted. With five minutes left for the voting, the three aforementioned people were still the lead candidates for the dunk tank.

More phone calls came in with votes and pleas and threats. In the last minute of the voting, Grace was approached by two Senior Executives waving a check with a large amount of money in favor of the President being chosen along with the HR person second, and she was told emphatically to shut it down that second or else. The President had already phoned in his large commitment to ensure that the HR Executive would be the pick.

The window for casting votes was closed, and the results were posted. Grace and everyone around her were aghast at what they had just witnessed and worried about what would happen the next day and how it would all play itself out.

Grace and her Hog Jaw team did not sleep very well that night, and they had an early call of duty to set up tables and chairs for the picnic lunch and greet the hot lunch vendor as well as the "Take the Plunge" vendor for setup and prep. It was a cooler than usual December day for Hog Jaw, sunny but with a rawness to it that spoke to the feeling Grace had had in her stomach since the day before. Today was the day of reckoning for Grace, her team, the campaign, and quite frankly for the company they worked for. Would this campaign end on a high note? Would the people's choices show up, or would this turn into a calamity of epic proportions?

After everything was set up outside and the food was being prepared, Grace and the team went back inside to spend some time doing their day jobs and finish final preparations for the lunch. Once Grace was back at her desk, she started to check her email, only to find that there were two messages of note. The first was a summons to the VP of HR's office, and the second one was from the admin for the president, stating that he had called in sick with a cold and would not be attending today's event, but that he had designated a substitute to stand in for him at the dunking. Seriously?

Grace promptly left her desk to make the two stops, one to HR and the second to find out who the substitute would be so that Grace could manage the expectations of the employees.

Needless to say, neither of these drop-bys were going to build her team spirit or confidence in how this day was going to eventually turnout.

When Grace approached the VP of HR's office, he asked her to come in and sit down before closing the door behind her. No time was spared or small talk exchanged before he asked bluntly, "How did this happen that I was voted in to be the plunge candidate?" Grace, unclear if she was in trouble and about to lose her job, replied, "Do you want to know the truth, or does it matter because I'm going to be fired anyway?" He said he wanted the truth and so Grace shared with him that the president himself had written one large check ensuring that the VP was the candidate. While not necessarily happy with her answer, he thanked her for being truthful, asked her not to share with anyone about this conversation, and told Grace that he came prepared to be dunked. Grace thanked him for his support and quickly left his office. Then Grace went to see the President's administrator to ask what today's plan B was going to be.

Shaking her head in disgust, she said that another male Senior Executive would be "Taking the Plunge" on behalf of the President and that he too was prepared for the tank.

Grace went back to her cube shaking, saddened, and repulsed by what she had encountered in the last twenty-four hours, as well as with the entire leadership team of her company, and she did her best to put on her game face, wishing that this day and this whole campaign would just be over. But, alas, it wasn't—there were still some serious plunges about to take place and more charity dollars to be raised.

Outside, everything was heating up but the weather with the first wave of lunches ready to be served and the first round of plunging candidates shivering in their swim trunks waiting to get soaked. It was two dollars a throw or three throws for five dollars. Team Leads were climbing in the tank while their direct reports were awaiting their turn trying to hit the target and watch them take the plunge. It was quite the spectacle to observe. Smiles on everyone's faces, picnic lunches, high fives, lots of softballs being sold, water getting splashed everywhere, and a feeling of team bonding that would never be matched again.

In the final half-hour of the "Take the Plunge" event, both of the chosen Senior Executives came out in their swim trunks with beach towels wrapped tightly around them in the cool December air. First was the brave VP of HR, taking one for the good of the cause and smiling as he climbed out because he had fun, did his duty, and finally knew his truth. He thanked Grace, shook her hand, and told her what a tremendous job she and the team had done throughout the whole campaign before heading back into the building to warm up from the cold.

Last to go in was the SVP designate. There was a look of surprise and a lot of murmuring in the crowd as the line was forming for employees to take their turn at plunging the president, but not a word was spoken. His absence said everything they needed to know.

READER PARTICIPATION & REFLECTION EXERCISES

"It is neither trials nor relationships, nor successes or failures that define a person, but the choices they make while handling them"

—RICHELLE E. GOODRICH

CHAPTER 9 LESSON: "SOMETIMES YOU CAN DO EVERYTHING RIGHT AND THINGS WILL STILL GO WRONG. THE KEY IS TO NEVER STOP DOING RIGHT."

—ANGIE THOMAS

1. How well did the six events the team ran support the five-pronged strategy of bringing it to the people, helping them understand why, using frequent communication, indelibly touching their hearts, and making it fun?

2. Sometimes you can do everything right and things will still go wrong. Where did things go wrong in this situation? What message did it send to Grace, her team, and all the employees? How do you bounce back from something like this in life?

3. What does it mean to have a failure of character? Who has the character flaw in this story: Grace or the leadership team? Why do you say that?

4. What are your character flaws that keep you from achieving your dreams?

Chapter 10

NEVER WRESTLE WITH A PIG

"Never wrestle with a pig because you'll
get dirty and the pig likes it."

—GEORGE BERNARD SHAW

To engage in a struggle with an opponent that benefits from the struggle even without winning it. Positive energy is much more powerful than negative energy. If you stay positive, the negative can't touch you.

The campaign was finally over, and the results were in. The goal was met: the fundraiser had its first time ever achievement of 100% participation in both locations. And they doubled the amount of money raised from the previous year. That's not ten thousand to twenty thousand but double a six figure number achieved, and most importantly no one from the team had gotten fired yet! It was time to celebrate the holidays and reward the best team ever, who went from last to first in just one short year, with an appropriate holiday team adventure.

The company was throwing a Christmas party in both locations, but Grace just felt that with everything the teams had been through and overcome in the past year they needed a special treat, so she had one last team meeting in Hog Jaw to wrap up the year and set the course for where they were going in the next one.

Grace decided that since they had spent the whole year talking about what they were building their houses out of, they should actually build one together. Not a real house, obviously, but one that would symbolize how far they'd come as a team and would bring joy to others in doing it. So they set an evening aside and volunteered at a charity house where sick children and their parents and siblings received free room and board while the children were treated for unimaginable illnesses. The activities: story time, karaoke, and building gingerbread houses with the families to make Christmas just a wee bit more fun under the circumstances they were in.

And being who they were now, they just had to split up and compete on who could build the prettiest house! In the end they were all uniquely beautiful just like the members of the team that built them.

Then, right before the children were to be tucked in for the evening, everyone on Grace's team as well as the children and their parents gathered in a circle for story time. In the spirit of everything the team had just been through that year, Grace opted out of a Christmas story and decided to read, once again, The Three Little Pigs. Everything was going so well, and Grace was happy but a bit weary from a long day and even longer year when suddenly, as she was reading the part about the houses being made of straw, sticks, and bricks, Grace got a bit tongue-tied.

Instead of sticks or bricks, Grace blurted out "A House made of Pricks." Everyone on the team as well as the parents burst out laughing while Grace turned blood red and giggled along with them. After that memorable moment, everyone went home with a smile on their face and a newly adopted team theme song in their heart, suggestion courtesy of Spamala: Sister Sledge "We Are Family."

The New Year came in with a bang as the company moved to new office space with a lot more room for expansion and growth. For reasons unknown to Grace or anyone else, R.E. Pigglesworth went "poof" and was no longer working for the company. So as anticipated the new year brought a fresh wave of chaos and uncertainty. Grace thought, *Here we go again!*

The first two months of the new year went by in a hurry with everyone getting settled into their new office space. Before long it became time for Grace to be introduced to her new boss, Oliver Snort, SVP of Sales, and to be given her annual review.

Oliver was a tall handsome man who had a kind manner about him and talked about his wife and children in their meeting. He wanted to know about Grace's family and her accomplishments during her first year. Grace had many accomplishments to share, stories of adventures and success with her team, and she was always happy to talk about family. What weighed heavily on Grace's mind, though, was whether that promise made a year ago by R.E. and then again six months later before the fundraising campaign would be kept.

Grace didn't have to wait long for the answer when she directly asked Oliver that very question. Oliver weighed in immediately, responding that he had not been made aware of any such commitment, but even if he had been, he wouldn't be comfortable without at least another six months of close observation of Grace in action before he could make that recommendation. There were new things he wanted her to learn and new people to add to her team until he could find them a new manager, but what he wanted to do was start setting up meetings with Grace, him, and other Senior Executives to get her more exposure and outline yet another yellow brick road to that year-old promise of a promotion.

Grace had no choice but to accept what she was being told, comply, and decide to move forward or move on out. Grace did let Oliver know that during the Christmas break her mom, who lived with her and who she took care of, was given only three to six more months to live, so there would probably be days when she might not be available as this was already well into month three and her mom still had not shared that news with her siblings.

On so many levels, Grace was devastated, and she had no recourse because everything R.E. had promised to occur was always verbal and not in writing. He was just let go, so who would believe her? The feeling of despondency was so heavy that it was very hard for Grace to breathe. Her mother was dying, and they just added more responsibility to her plate, more people to manage, more new things to incorporate, and a new person to prove herself to, sadly with no respect or acknowledgement for what Grace and her team had accomplished. On the bright side, at least she was now reporting directly to a SVP that was going to include her in senior management meetings and decisions.

Although once again Grace did not hear the news she was hoping to hear, she decided to keep moving forward, keep her reports on track, and not let negativity set in for her or her team. Whatever came their way as a team, they would make the most of it with everything they had.

THE INVITATION

With "back to business as usual" being the order of the days ahead, Grace and team continued excelling at their work. With all the enhanced relationships they had built during the campaign, they were able to resolve issues, prevent problems from happening, and provide the clients they served excellent growth opportunities. Grace was pleased.

Grace then received an invitation to attend the fundraising charity's community awards banquet with an opportunity to bring seven other guests. It was suggested that Grace might want someone from Senior Leadership to attend with her, so she extended the invitation as requested. To no one's surprise on Grace's team, all the invitations to Senior Leadership came back as a no, so Grace invited her Hog Jaw team and a few other key players that helped with the project to go with her to the luncheon.

On the day of the luncheon, everyone decided to dress to win, even though they were rookies at this and just figured they were getting a half-day off and a nice free lunch in recognition for their efforts, more than what they had gotten from their own company. In reality, they simply expected to be recognized for achieving the goal of a hundred percent participation, and perhaps for the dollar growth they achieved by doubling the donations, as Grace had seen previous similar awards encased on the floor where all the executive offices were. So they chatted away, enjoying the meal, the company, and the time away from the office.

When the award ceremony began, Grace and her team watched as awards were presented to companies in groupings based on number of employees and size of the company, which seemed a fair way to do it. When their company's size grouping was mentioned, they were in fact recognized for achieving the goal of one hundred percent participation, as well as the one hundred percent growth in contribution year over year, with plaques that could be added to the company's glass trophy case. These were symbols to take back and to display that their reputation in the community was preserved for yet another year.

Things were winding down at the banquet, with only a few awards left to give, when the last award was announced. This award was the most coveted of all because it was for Campaign Chairperson of the Year and spanned across companies both smaller and much larger than Grace and the team's. They were not even paying that much attention as they were too busy brooding that the fun and games of the day were over and it was still early enough that they might have to go back to the office.

And then it happened! The female CEO of the charity announced, "The Campaign Chairperson of the Year Award goes to Grace Fully for her outstanding commitment, creativity, appreciation and comprehension of our mission, results, and poise under pressure. Grace, will you please come forward to receive your award!" Everyone at the table stood up and cheered, hugged, high-fived each other, and cried. No one ever saw that one coming, especially Grace. The entire banquet hall stood, clapped, and cheered for Grace and her teammates as she stepped forward to receive her hard-earned award. Grace shook hands with the CEO of the charity, hugged her charity ambassador, and raised the award in the air for her team to see and know that they had indeed just now taken flight. Grace would tell her team when they returned to the office later that she swore she saw a pig with wings and a cape flying over that ballroom and all the way back to the office with them that day.

After settling in, Grace knew that she had one last task to complete that day, and that was to take the awards up to the office of the CEO for the display case. The charity had already called Petunia and let her know about the awards, so she was not surprised when Grace came to her door carrying the goods. She sheepishly commented that she regretted that no Senior-Level person was there to witness what had happened on the company's behalf that day, and she acknowledged the team for its effort as she grabbed the keys to head over to put the hardware in the display case. Grace first handed her the award for one hundred percent participation, and then the award for one hundred percent growth year over year, but when she reached for the Chairperson of the Year award to place on the shelf, Grace confidently looked at her and said, "I believe this one has my name on it, and it belongs to me and my team." Then she turned and walked away.

> **See Ground Rules:** 1, 2, 3, 4, 5, & 6! Stay true to who you are. Practice what you preach. Love your team. Stand up for them and show your strength, courage and fortitude. Always put their success before your own. And if necessary, be willing to take a bullet for them to earn their trust—that way, they know you aren't asking them to do something you wouldn't do yourself. The bullet in this case was to Grace's future career there as she rightfully claimed her team's trophy for their own.

READER PARTICIPATION & REFLECTION EXERCISES

"Yes, victory is sweet, but it doesn't make life any easier the next season or even the next day."

—PHIL JACKSON

CHAPTER 10 LESSON: TAKE YOUR VICTORIES WHERE YOU CAN GET THEM.

1. What is the great irony of Chapter 10?

2. What did building the gingerbread houses at the children's charity signify to the team about how far they'd come that year?

3. How did Grace's handling of the award trophies with the CEO signify to her that she was also a force to be reckoned with? How do you
   think she took it? What did it say about Grace and her team? How
   would you handle yourself in that situation?

4. Does the story really end here? What do you think demonstrating
   strength, leadership, and accomplishment resulted in for Grace and
   her team for the future?

A PIG'S TALE

If I were going to grow up and be something
I think I'd want to be a pig!
Why on earth would you want to do that?
When you could be something BIG!!
Pigs can be fat and sure get dirty.
Pigs are quite smelly and not very purty.
But there's something about pigs that most folks won't buy.
Not only can pigs walk and swim, they've also been known to fly!

How can that be when they can't lift off the ground?
They can and they will when their flight plan is quite sound.
The way to cultivate that high functioning team,
Remember as you manage, let the light on them beam.
Go with them in battle and stand up for what's right,
Take the bumps and the bruises and when endangered be willing to bite!
Nurture and support them and celebrate every success,
And they'll deliver like champions when the mantra, "Do more with Less!"

Like the ten little piggies on your hands and toes,
Each team member brings a skill set, when yours might run low.
Bring out their beauty by touching their heart,
And remember you're stronger as a team than anyone can be apart.
Have faith and they will deliver when they know what to expect.
Teach them how to handle disappointments, when things don't go perfect!
It's a simple flight plan that I know to be true.
And if you follow it closely, your team can fly too!

—GRACE FULLY

SUMMARY

After completing the first draft of this story, I had the privilege to speak to a friend of mine who is a pilot and ask him to dumb down for me in English exactly what the concept of a flight plan is, what it's used for, and why it's necessary to have on every flight. My goal was to determine if the main character, Grace, without any flight training or knowledge, had truly set forth a plan for her team to follow such that if theoretically pigs could fly, they had been given everything they needed to be successful and get to their destination.

The way he explained it to me was that every flight required a flight plan to be filed before take-off. The reason, as he explained, is to have an insurance policy in case something goes wrong, meaning you have let someone know in advance where you are going and how you plan to get there.

The process actually begins by calling a Flight Service Station (FSS) to obtain a weather briefing for your intended destination and route of flight. After you understand the conditions you'll be flying in, then you file your flight plan with the FSS as a guide, giving the information on the plan in sequential order.

Once you file your flight plan, you then have to activate it. One way of doing this is to contact FSS once you are airborne. Once you reach your destination, you have to close your flight by calling FSS on the phone or the radio.

The last step is critical because if they don't hear from you within thirty minutes of your estimated time of arrival by radio, things will escalate progressively, becoming more intense up to the activation of search and rescue efforts.

Thanks, Captain Gil Barrera!

U.S. DEPARTMENT OF TRANSPORTATION FEDERAL AVIATION ADMINISTRATION **FLIGHT PLAN**	(FAA USE ONLY) ☐ PILOT BRIEFING ☐ VNR ☐ STOPOVER		TIME STARTED	SPECIALIST INITIALS

1. TYPE ☐ VFR ☐ IFR ☐ DVFR	2. AIRCRAFT IDENTIFICATION	3. AIRCRAFT TYPE/ SPECIAL EQUIPMENT	4. TRUE AIRSPEED KTS	5. DEPARTURE POINT	6. DEPARTURE TIME PROPOSED (Z) | ACTUAL (Z)	7. CRUISING ALTITUDE

8. ROUTE OF FLIGHT

9. DESTINATION (Name of airport and city)	10. EST. TIME ENROUTE HOURS | MINUTES	11. REMARKS

12. FUEL ON BOARD HOURS | MINUTES	13. ALTERNATE AIRPORT(S)	14. PILOT'S NAME, ADDRESS & TELEPHONE NUMBER & AIRCRAFT HOME BASE	15. NUMBER ABOARD
		17. DESTINATION CONTACT/TELEPHONE (OPTIONAL)	

16. COLOR OF AIRCRAFT	CIVIL AIRCRAFT PILOTS. FAR 91 requires you file an IFR flight plan to operate under instrument flight controlled airspace. Failure to file could result in a civil penalty not to exceed $1,000 for each violation (Sec Federal Aviation Act of 1958, as amended). Filing of a VFR flight plan is recommended as a good operating Part 99 for requirements concerning DVFR flight plans.

FAA Form 7233-1 (8-82)   CLOSE VFR FLIGHT PLAN WITH _____ FSS ON ARRIVAL

I will let my readers decide for themselves if Grace clearly laid out for her team the conditions which they were working under and the route they were taking to achieve their mission, activated the plan in full force in both locations, and closed the flight by getting to the destination called phenomenal success! Grace believed these pigs could fly, but I think the evidence is more than compelling to indicate that not only did they fly, they soared.

ACKNOWLEDGEMENTS

A Pig's Tale was actually first drafted about eight years ago and then was mysteriously locked in and not accessible for some unknown reason on my antique computer that I have refused to let go.

As I began the New Year of 2023 I found myself a bit sad, uncertain, and uncomfortable with the concept of retirement and how I might fill my days not just with stuff but with activities that had meaning and purpose. So I called upon a friend, a young man of about thirty, that I mentor from time to time, Brandon Forschino, and asked him to meet me for coffee. We met and the next thing you know I was crying to him that my life had no purpose now that I wasn't working.

Brandon quickly and proudly took control of the situation and turned mentor on me and I left that coffee date with a homework assignment of epic proportions which was to document all the milestones in my life that have made me the person I am today. I had sixty three years to ponder and let me tell you it was an enlightening, lengthy, and at times a painful process. When I completed it we met again and I summarized for him what I learned about myself and then he entitled it "My Life's Truth's". Then Brandon said " These are the things you now focus on and find activities to share your wealth of experience in."

About a month later out of the blue I got a call from a local business that had an active women's group called Women4Women that asked me if I'd consider speaking to their group about my first book, the Sno Cone

Diaries. Somehow when they sent me a Google document to complete detailing the outline of my speech, the manuscript for A Pig's Tale appeared in all its glory! I have no other answer for it other than "Divine Intervention." Thank you Vivianne, Katherine, and Carrie for unlocking all that was lost, and the opportunity to speak to your beautiful group of women.

Then I was invited by a new friend I had made in the mountains, Carol Applegate, to come and visit her in Carmel, Indiana. Little did I know she would hold a luncheon in my honor and all of her friends were authors. She also had a niece that has a pig for a pet that we promptly called and I interviewed her for over an hour. The niece, not the pig named Kevin Bacon. You can't make this stuff up. Thank you Carol Applegate for your awesome hospitality, and for the introduction to your niece, Dr. Amy Bixler. She has helped me with understanding some things about life, stress, and pigs, and from those conversations we have become good friends.

I also want to thank Isabel Steiner Carol's granddaughter, who at age twelve was so taken when I told the story of Christopher, from my first book Sno Cone Diaries to her family, and the idea for my new book, A Pig's Tale, that she made several drawings of flying pigs for me before I left. I am proud to feature one of those drawings in the front of the book. She wants to be an artist someday so I told her I'd give her that first shot at having her work published. You are a beautiful soul Izzie, don't ever stop believing in yourself. Avery, (her brother) is pretty smart and awesome too despite cheering for questionable football teams. I love spending time with you both.

Now that I was committed to finishing and publishing A Pig's Tale and wanted to do a ten year update on Sno Cone Diaries, I set out to find a new publisher since mine had taken ill and could not help me anymore. Like anyone, I Googled publishers, read the reviews, and took a shot and made a phone appointment with one called Palmetto Publishing. When my contact there told me that she was so moved by my Sno Cone story about Christopher that she emailed me details of her own personal story, and I knew then I'd found the right publisher. Thank you Brandy! When Brandy left and turned my work over to Grace, I knew for certain I was in the right place for The Sno Cone Diaries is now more beautiful than I could have ever imagined and Grace is now part of launching Grace Fully's A Pig's Tale.

Then Carol Applegate invited me to participate and speak at her Voice of Aging Conference in Carmel Indiana, in October. After we spoke of aging, dementia, disabilities, shared real intense caregiving stories, how to survive being a caregiver , the cost of housing as you age, the legal and financial planning that needs to be done so you don't run out of money before you die and that your dying wishes are actually met, I was charged with the small task of cheering everyone up. My real presentation was entitled "The Monkey on Everyone's Back", but Carol told everyone that I was going to tell everyone how I taught pigs how to fly. So with everyone's blessing I told a joke involving a pig, a monkey, and poop, and that's how I weaved those topics together to make everyone laugh. The story of my life, making something out of nothing. Thanks Carol for allowing me to be part of the seminar. But a big shout out to my friend and former co-worker Heather Pouncey for driving over from Columbus Ohio to Carmel, Indiana just to hear me speak.

I also want to thank my husband Juan, our daughter Alexis and her husband Travis who gave me sweet Dorothy to love on as a first grandchild, Justin our son and his girlfriend Reed. They are my love and inspiration to be everything I can be no matter how crazy it may sound to them at the time. They have learned to go with the flow that mom is in, let her embrace it, and give love in her own special way. I love you always and all our travel adventures and the memories we make.

Thank you Stephanie, Trish, Carol, Heather, Brandon, and Amy for reading A Pig's Tale and giving me so much of your time, thoughts, and honest feedback to make the story better.

Thank you Karen Shields for inviting me to cook at our local homeless shelter, Mission House and supporting me at my speech at Women4Women, and at the First Annual Cookies with Claus giving homemade Christmas cookies to the homeless. What an incredible gift that day was for me and getting to meet and speak with "Johnny."

And last but not least thank you Nick & Kirsten, Ed & Joan, John & Cathy, and John & Laurie for being our cheerleaders, go to travel buddies, mountain friends, and Saturday night out dinner companions, and special occasion celebrants etc… We always have so much fun together.

And lastly Joan, thank you for giving me the opportunity to assume the role of Mrs. Claus for the 25th edition of the Children's Christmas Party of Jacksonville and its almost 5,000 children that receive gifts. Having Alexis and Dorothy as my elves and capturing that moment forever, along with meeting Santa, and hugging, smiling, welcoming, and taking pictures with all those children brought me the greatest joy of the year.

When I reflect back on 2023 and how it started with me being sad with no purpose and ended with me being Mrs. Claus, all I can say is" WOW" and I can't wait to see where my adventures and truths take me in 2024!

LOVE YOU ALL!

ABBY

APPENDIX:

BIBLIOGRAPHY:

https://en.m.wikipedia.org/wiki/The_Chicken_And_The_Pig

www.blog.klm.com

www.phrases.org.uk/meanings/a-pig-in-a-poke

https://en.wikipedia.org/wiki/Lipstick_on_a_pig

https://en.m.wikipedia.org/wiki/The_Three_Little_Pigs

https://www.merriamwebster.com

https://www.networkforgood.com

https://www.dictionary.com

www.https://en.m.wiktionary.org

https://studyfinds.org>bizarre-dreams

https://a-zanimals.org

OUTLINE OF MAIN CHARACTERS

Name	Title
Petunia Squiggles	CEO
Barley Cunnigham	President
Oliver Snort	Sr. VP of Sales
Suey Oinker	VP of Operations
R. E. Pigglesworth	Vice President of Sales
Grace Fully	Manager
Babe Alicious	Sales Rep/Team Lead, Hawg Jaw
Chris P. Bacon	Sales Rep
Elvis Pigsly	Sales Rep
Spamala Anderson	Sales Rep
Piggy Azalea	Sales Rep
Pork Chop	Jr. Sales Rep
Guinea Stefani	Sales Rep/Team Lead, Hawg Dawg
Ava Ga Boar	Sales Rep
Taylor Swine	Sales Rep
Barbie Que	Sales Rep
Pig Achu	Jr. Sales Rep
Dixie Stardust	Executive Trainer

FOURTEEN INTERESTING AND FUN FACTS ABOUT PIGS

1. Pigs are very social animals and like to seek the company of others. They often dream and like to sleep nose to nose to make sure they are touching their friends.

2. Pigs are considered to be the third most intelligent animal, behind apes and whales. They have the cognitive ability to be smarter than a dog or a three-year-old human.

3. Pigs have a highly developed sense of smell and have been used in battle to sniff out landmines. They also locate expensive truffles.

4. Pigs can be trained to do many tasks and tricks.

5. Pigs are excellent swimmers.

6. Pigs are fast and can run up to eleven miles per hour.

7. Pigs can squeal very loudly, sometimes up to 115 decibels, three decibels higher than a supersonic jet.

8. Pigs do not have sweat glands. That's the reason they roll around in the mud—to stay cool.

9. Despite the stigma, pigs actually prefer cleanliness.

10. Pigs are thirsty creatures, consuming up to fourteen gallons of water a day.

11. Pigs have an excellent sense of direction. Pigs are navigators, and they can find their way home over large distances.

12. Pigs have exceptional memories, especially when it comes to object location—like where they will find great food.

13. Pigs are sentient beings, meaning they experience a wide range of emotions and can feel pain.

14. Pigs are a bit OCD about food and will do just about anything to get it.

IN MEMORIAM

GERALDINE W. HOLTER
10/1/1938 – 11/23/2022

This is one of the earliest memories I have as a child: being a flower girl in my aunt and godmother's wedding in May of 1963. I was about three and a half years old at the time, and if memory serves me correctly, I was just getting over a case of the measles. The other distinct memory I have of this same occasion is my dad giving me a bath the night before while singing "Get Me to the Church On Time" by Frederick Loewe from the 1956 musical *My Fair Lady*.

Aunt Gerry was truly "My Fair Lady!" The word "fair" has multiple definitions, like impartial and just, without favoritism, and a beautiful woman. In her case, she was all of them— except without a doubt I was her favorite, or at least that's how she made me feel whenever I was with her. At the wedding, she and Uncle Al taught me my first dance, the "Twist!" She took me grocery shopping with my grandmother Busia every week on her day off, and we always ended our adventure with lunch at a department store that had the best clown ice cream cones I ever had!

As I grew older, she adopted two of her own children. After she taught me how to drive, in the summers I would go and live with them and babysit her kids, taking them to the pool and picking them up from various activities. She took me on various vacations with her family to places like Virginia Beach, Arkansas, and the Great Smoky Mountains. I loved seeing new places with them.

She was a dedicated RN from 1959 until she retired in 2017. Almost every ailment for me and my siblings was diagnosed and treated by a phone call to Aunt Gerry and the wonderful doctor she worked for, Dr. Cliff Ratliff.

Sadly, as I grew older life, children, jobs, and other circumstances took me away from home in Maryland to Florida. We didn't get to see each other as much, but she and Uncle Al did make at least one trip to Florida to see my family and where I lived.

Like everyone I know, she wasn't perfect. However, what I'd like to share with everyone is that she by far and away had the greatest impact on how I've led my life, why I've tried as hard as I have, and how I've overcome so many obstacles. She showed me by example that hard work would pay off for me in the end. She didn't miss a birthday, graduation, bridal or baby shower, and she even rescued our wedding when my own church wouldn't marry us on a Friday night but her church and Fr. Brian Rafferty would.

I attended her celebration of life service on May 4, 2023. It's hard to imagine not being able to pick up the phone and just call her anymore. One of the last conversations I had with her was when I shared the news that I had become a first-time grandmother in December of 2021. She was overjoyed for me, and neither of us could believe how so much time had passed so quickly.

I hope she is at peace now and that she and Uncle Al, aka Fred & Ginger, get to dance their hearts out every night with their parents and siblings all reunited in heaven again. I love you, Aunt Gerry, and thank you for every little thing you did to make my life just a little bit better.

WITH LOVE AND GRATITUDE!
ABBY

ABOUT THE AUTHOR:

A Pig's Tale: Survival Is As Much A Matter Of Grace As Fight is Abby Vega's second published work. It follows Sno-Cone Diaries: A Sweet Route To Happiness. This story has been many years in the making and she is thrilled to be able to share it with everyone at this time.

In her successful and accomplished career as an executive sales, marketing, management and training professional she has played a role in securing incredible outcomes for herself, her team members, clients, companies and businesses, and now she wants to share the six ground rules again with you.

SIX GROUND RULES OF LEADERSHIP

1. Stay True To Who You Are

2. Practice What You Preach

3. Love Your Team

4. Stand Up For Them and Show Your Strength, Courage and Fortitude

5. Always Put Their Success Before Your Own

6. And if Necessary, Be Willing To Take a Bullet For Them to Earn Their Trust. That Way. They Know You Aren't Asking Them to Do Something You Wouldn't Do Yourself.

The Six Ground Rules of Leadership was in this case Grace's flight plan to leading her team to achieve things they never thought possible, especially in light of where they were starting from. Add in a little MAGIC (believing in yourself) and see just how far you can go. You may even fly!

Abby Vega is a motivational speaker and the author. She lectures and does workshops on the topics of leadership, culture, sales, and teamwork, She holds a Master's Degree from Johns Hopkins University and a B.S. from Towson State University in business. Abby has lived in Ponte Vedra Beach, Florida for over twenty seven years with her husband of thirty-five years, Juan. Daughter Alexis, son-in-law Travis, and first grandchild Dorothy live in Brooklyn, New York now but will be moving to Buffalo, New York in the spring to work on the Buffalo Bill's new stadium. Go Jaguars!

Son Justin lives in Atlanta, Georgia.

Milton Keynes UK
Ingram Content Group UK Ltd.
UKHW020958010424
440417UK00008B/43